D0578659

Better Homes and Gardens®

# A Cross-Stitch CHRISTMAS®

## Heartfelt Holidays

This Book Belongs to:

Better Homes and Gardens ®
Des Moines, Iowa

**Better Homes and Gardens®**

# *A Cross-Stitch* CHRISTMAS®

Editor-in-Chief *Beverly Rivers*
Managing Editor *Julie Burch Keith*
Art Director *Patricia Church Podlasek*

*A Cross-Stitch Christmas®* Editor *Eve Mahr*

*Cross-Stitch & Needlework®* Editor *Nancy R. Wyatt*
Assistant Art Director *Cherie DeTolve-Dale*
Associate Editor/Crafts Group *Barbara Hickey*
Editorial Assistant *Mary Johnson*
Illustrators *Chris Neubauer Graphics, Glenda Aldrich, Barbara Gordon*
Photographers *Perry Struse, Marcia Cameron*

Publisher *William R. Reed*
Advertising/Marketing Director *Maureen Ruth*
Business Manager *Janet Donnelly*
Marketing Manager *Andre Okolowitz*
Promotions Supervisor *M. Max Wilker*
Sales/Marketing Assistant *Kristi Hasek*

Vice President, Publishing Director *Jerry Ward*

Chairman and CEO *William T. Kerr*

Chairman of the Executive Committee
*E.T. Meredith III*

Meredith Publishing Group
Publishing Group President *Christopher M. Little*
Strategic Marketing *Bill Murphy*
Finance *Max Runciman*
Controller *Karla Jeffries*
Licensing and New Media *Thomas L. Slaughter*
Consumer Marketing *Hal Oringer*
Operations *Dean Pieters*
Creative Services *Ellen de Lathouder*

Our "Mark of Excellence" seal assures you that every project in this publication has been constructed and checked under the direction of the crafts experts at Better Homes and Gardens® *Cross Stitch & Needlework®* magazine.

**For book editorial questions,** write *Better Homes and Gardens® Cross Stitch & Needlework®*, 1716 Locust St.–GA 311, Des Moines, IA 50309-3023; phone 515/284-3623; fax 515/284-3884.


First Edition. Printing Number and Year: 5 4 3 2 1 03 02 01 00 99

ISSN: 1081-468X
ISBN: 0-696-20958-6

*The magic of Christmas inspires us to celebrate the season. Suddenly, we have an impassioned drive to make our homes warm and inviting places and to seek uniquely pleasing gifts for everyone on our lists. When cross-stitchers create holiday gifts and decorations, we rely on our fingers—and our hearts—to stitch special treasures that spread Christmas to everyone. With such thoughts in mind, the editors of* Cross Stitch and Needlework® *magazine filled this book with projects for you to work with love. Designers from around the world created wonderful wall hangings, super stockings, oodles of ornaments, and gifts galore. As always, we chose designs to touch your heart. We also wanted to stimulate your creative instincts, so we added lots of extra pieces and ideas to help you accomplish your own*

*Heartfelt Holidays.*

Page 77

# Contents

Page 14

Page 16

Page 33

Page 52

Page 116

Page 48

Page 32

Page 35

# *The Spirit*

# *of the Season*

*Christmas evokes a host of memories: a child's starry eyes, the fragrance of fir trees, the satiny feel of ribbon, and the harmony of carols. When cross-stitchers capture these images on fabric, they become lasting symbols to share with future generations.*

A 15th-century carol, "Lo, How a Rose Ere Blooming," compares the perfection of the Christ Child to roses with their sweet fragrance and tender blooms. Capture the beauty of roses in lush holiday projects—like a richly colored bouquet, *opposite,* dramatically set against black 25-count Lugana and embellished with sparkling beads and golden ribbons. Stitch the whole design to grace a lined oak box that's perfect for Christmas treasures. For a smaller gift, choose a single rose, *above,* stitched in shades of yellow on 18-count ice blue damask Aida cloth, and finish it as a classic broach with year-round appeal.

*Design: Barbara Sestok*

Long before the story of Christmas was written on paper, angels were part of it. Today, as then, they symbolize peace and good news in literature and music. The delicacy of this silver-winged messenger, wearing flowing robes and carrying a mandolin, is enhanced by petite cross-stitch face and hands.

More than a century ago, Queen Victoria popularized the Christmas tree, aglow with candles and blown-glass baubles. Today, twinkling electric lights have replaced candles, and we spread ornaments throughout the house—on wreaths, table tops, and mantels. This old-fashioned ball trim, stitched on gold-flecked Aida cloth, glitters atop a shiny brass trinket jar. For a more traditional approach, mount to hang it on the tree.

*Designs: Angel, Mary Kay Werning; ornament, Barbara Sestok*

Celebrating the 12 days of Christmas that stretch from Christmas Day to Epiphany, January 6, is an English custom celebrated in a popular song. Stitch these first-day symbols, *above*—golden pears and a plump partridge nestled in a wreath of verdant holly—to enjoy throughout the holidays.

Here's a new twist on the traditional basket of Christmas cheer, *opposite*. Stitched in soft colors and embellished with appealing scrollwork, this collection of holiday goodies will last for years.

*Designs: Pear wreath, Barbara Sestok; basket, Anne Cook translated by Barbara Sestok*

MERRY
CHRISTMAS

Take a natural approach to holiday decorating. Brighten a mantel with an elegant stitched arch of apples, grapes, holly, and mistletoe. Then, follow the theme of fruit and greens in an impromptu arrangement of natural materials. Or, position the arch over the doorway with a few fir branches and a sprig of mistletoe to encourage holiday affection.

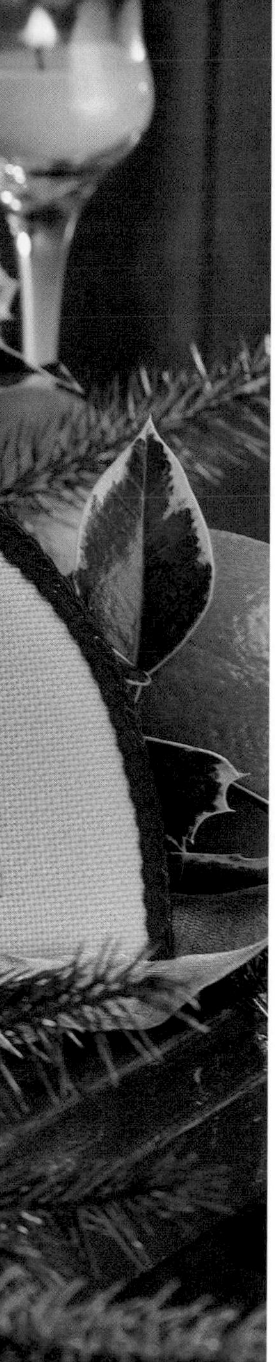

When the subject comes from nature, just one small ornament—with a few natural props—fills a table top. For example, this small fruit and holly design tucks neatly into a pretty basket or bowl with apples, pears, a few sprigs of greenery, and shiny ribbon.

*Designs: Barbara Sestok*

In the span of 100 years, poinsettias, with their showy green-and-scarlet foliage, evolved from wild shrubs growing only in California, Mexico, and Central America to the most popular of all holiday plants. Accent this wreath of festive blooms with a fluffy ruffle of touchable velveteen.

*Design: Barbara Sestok*

## Roses Box

### Supplies

*12" square of 25-count black Lugana fabric*
*Cotton embroidery floss*
*Kreinik blending filament*
*Mill Hill seed beads*
*7" square oak box with 5¼" square design area*
*7" square of fleece*
*Spray adhesive*

### Stitches

Center and stitch the chart using three plies of floss unless otherwise specified. Press from the back.

### Assembly

Remove the mounting board from the lid of the box. Spray it lightly with adhesive. Press the fleece onto the adhesive. Assemble according to directions included with the box.

## Yellow Rose Pin

### Supplies

*8" square of 18-count ice blue damask Aida cloth*
*Cotton embroidery floss*
*3×4" piece each of tracing paper, fleece, self-stick mounting board with foam, and white felt*
*Erasable fabric marker*
*14" piece of ⅞"-wide lace*
*Crafts glue*
*1¼"-long pin back*
*All-purpose adhesive*

ROSE PIN
Fold
Fold

### Stitches

Center and stitch the rose motif (indicated on the chart by a dashed blue line) using two plies of floss for cross-stitches and one ply for backstitches. Press from the back.

### Assembly

Fold the tracing paper into quarters. Aligning folds, trace the pattern, *above;* cut out. Unfold the pattern and use it to cut one shape *each* from the fleece, mounting board, and felt.

Peel the protective paper from the mounting board. Center the foam side

*Continued*

### *Roses Box*

| Anchor | DMC |
|---|---|
| 013 | 349 Coral |
| 310 | 434 Medium chestnut |
| 266 | 471 Avocado |
| 305 | 725 Topaz |
| 307 | 783 Christmas gold |
| 380 | 838 Beige-brown |
| 246 | 986 Forest green |
| 292 | 3078 Lemon |
| 267 | 3346 Hunter green |
| 266 | 3347 Medium yellow-green |
| 264 | 3348 Light yellow-green |
| 035 | 3705 Dark watermelon |
| 033 | 3706 Medium watermelon |
| 1015 | 3777 Terra-cotta |
| 874 | 3822 Straw |
| BACKSTITCH (1X) | |
| 310 | 434 Medium chestnut – bittersweet stems |
| 264 | 3348 Light yellow-green – leaf veins |
| 874 | 3822 Straw – bittersweet |
| | 002 Kreinik Gold #4 very fine braid – ribbon |
| | 005 Kreinik Black #4 very fine braid – roses |
| | 015 Kreinik Chartreuse #4 very fine braid – leaves |

SEED BEADS
00165 Mill Hill Christmas red seed beads – bittersweet berries

***Roses and Ribbon Box Stitch count:*** *59 high x 59 wide*

***Finished design sizes:***
*25-count fabric – 4¾ x 4¾ inches*
*28-count fabric – 4¼ x 4¼ inches*
*32-count fabric – 3⅝ x 3⅝ inches*

***Yellow Rose Ornament Stitch count:*** *34 high x 46 wide*

***Finished design sizes:***
*18-count fabric – 1⅞ x 2½ inches*
*16-count fabric – 2⅛ x 2⅞ inches*
*14-count fabric – 2⅜ x 3¼ inches*

### *Yellow Rose Pin*

| Anchor | DMC |
|---|---|
| 266 | 471 Avocado |
| 305 | 725 Topaz |
| 307 | 783 Christmas gold |
| 380 | 838 Beige-brown |
| 246 | 986 Forest green |
| 292 | 3078 Lemon |
| 267 | 3346 Hunter green |
| 266 | 3347 Medium yellow-green |
| 264 | 3348 Light yellow-green |
| 874 | 3822 Straw |
| BACKSTITCH (1X) | |
| 218 | 319 Pistachio – leaves |
| 358 | 433 Dark chestnut – roses |
| 264 | 3348 Light yellow-green – leaf veins |

Face - over one
Right Hand - over one

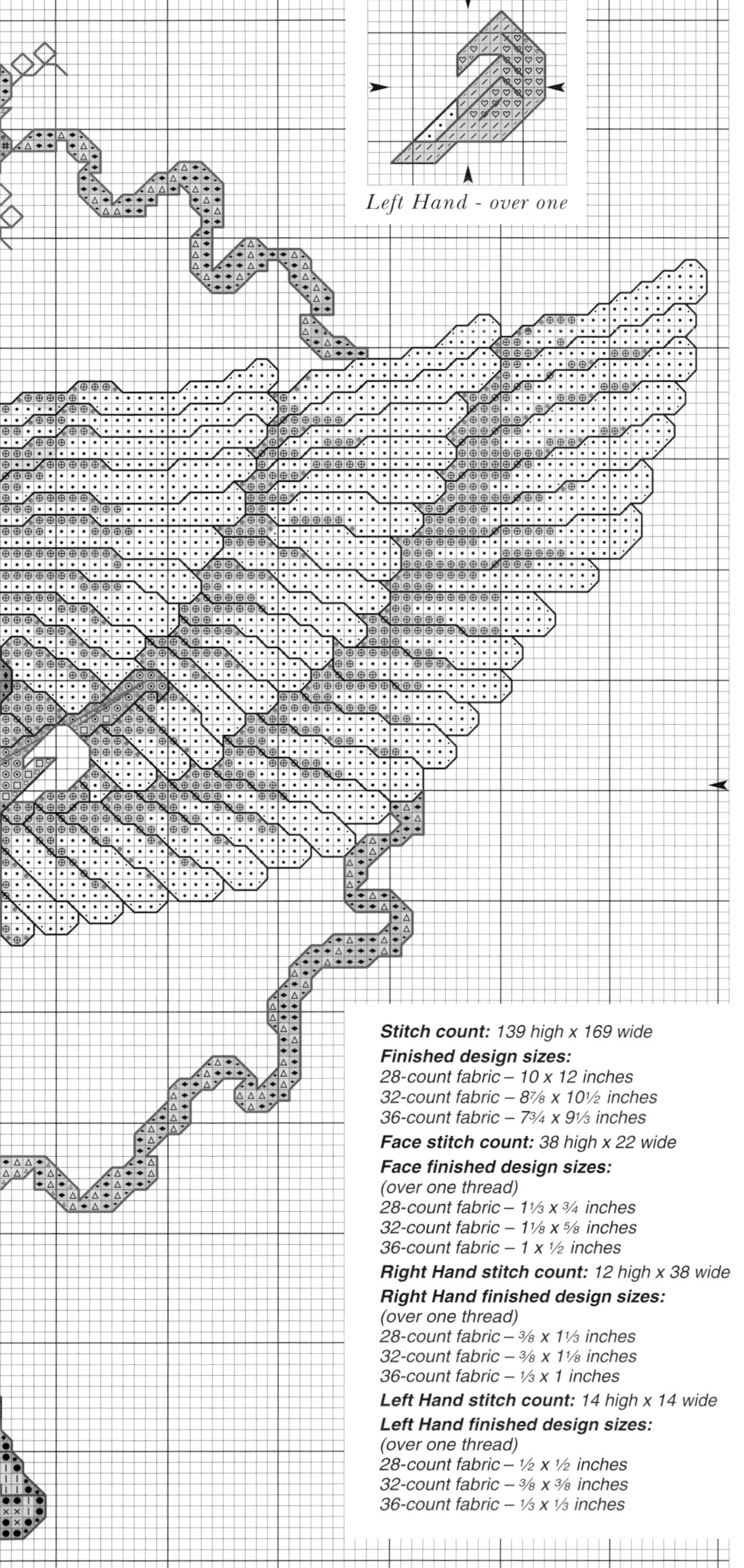

*Left Hand - over one*

***Stitch count:*** *139 high x 169 wide*

***Finished design sizes:***
*28-count fabric – 10 x 12 inches*
*32-count fabric – 8⅞ x 10½ inches*
*36-count fabric – 7¾ x 9⅓ inches*

***Face stitch count:*** *38 high x 22 wide*

***Face finished design sizes:***
*(over one thread)*
*28-count fabric – 1⅓ x ¾ inches*
*32-count fabric – 1⅛ x ⅝ inches*
*36-count fabric – 1 x ½ inches*

***Right Hand stitch count:*** *12 high x 38 wide*

***Right Hand finished design sizes:***
*(over one thread)*
*28-count fabric – ⅜ x 1⅓ inches*
*32-count fabric – ⅜ x 1⅛ inches*
*36-count fabric – ⅓ x 1 inches*

***Left Hand stitch count:*** *14 high x 14 wide*

***Left Hand finished design sizes:***
*(over one thread)*
*28-count fabric – ½ x ½ inches*
*32-count fabric – ⅜ x ⅜ inches*
*36-count fabric – ⅓ x ⅓ inches*

on the fleece; press to stick. Center the fleece side of the mounting board on the back of the stitched design. Trim the stitched fabric ⅝" beyond the edge of the mounting board. Fold the excess fabric to the back and glue.

Sew a row of gathering stitches along the straight edge of the lace. Pull threads, adjusting gathers evenly to fit the circumference of the pin. Use crafts glue to attach the lace to the back of the pin, beginning and ending at the center bottom. Glue felt to the back of the pin. Use all-purpose adhesive to glue the pin back to the felt.

## *Angel with Mandolin*

| Anchor | | DMC |
|---|---|---|
| 110 | ♦ | 208 Dark lavender |
| 109 | + | 209 Medium lavender |
| 108 | ○ | 210 Light lavender |
| 342 | \ | 211 Pale lavender |
| 1026 | / | 225 Pale shell pink |
| 117 | I | 341 Light periwinkle |
| 310 | ⊙ | 434 Medium chestnut |
| 1045 | □ | 436 Dark tan |
| 210 | ◆ | 562 Medium seafoam |
| 208 | △ | 563 True seafoam |
| 178 | ● | 791 Deep cornflower blue |
| 177 | × | 792 Dark cornflower blue |
| 175 | ◇ | 794 Light cornflower blue |
| 359 | ▲ | 801 Coffee brown |
| 271 | ♡ | 819 Pink |
| 244 | # | 987 Forest green |
| 120 | ∿ | 3747 Pale periwinkle |
| 1009 | – | 3770 Ivory |
| BLENDED NEEDLE | | |
| 002 | • | 000 White (2X) and 032 Pearl filament (1X) |
| 398 | ⊕ | 415 Pearl gray (2X) and 001HL Silver filament (1X) |
| 361 | ✳ | 738 Light tan (2X) and 002HL Gold filament (1X) |
| BACKSTITCH (1X) | | |
| 897 | / | 221 Deep shell pink – mouth and lips |
| 358 | / | 433 Dark chestnut - arm, hands, eyebrows, nose, chin |
| 102 | / | 550 Violet - shawl, hair ribbon |
| 178 | / | 791 Deep cornflower blue - gown, flowers |
| 244 | / | 987 Forest green - ribbon, tendrils |
| 382 | / | 3371 Black-brown - mandolin, hair, eyelids |
| 236 | / | 3799 Charcoal - wings |
| STRAIGHT STITCH (1X) | | |
| | / | 002P Kreinik gold cable - mandolin strings, necklace |
| MILL HILL BEADS | | |
| | ✕ | 00557 Gold seed bead - necklace |
| | ✕ | 13004 Light sapphire AB Margarita with 42011 Victorian gold petite bead |
| | ✕ | 13009 Heliotrope Margarita with 42011 Victorian gold petite bead |

## Angel with Mandolin

*The chart and key are on pages 18–19.*

**Supplies**

*22×24" piece of 28-count raw linen Cashel linen*
*Cotton embroidery floss*
*Kreinik metallic threads*
*Mill Hill seed beads and Crystal Treasures*
*Desired frame*

**Stitches**

Center and stitch the chart on the fabric. Use three plies of floss to work cross-stitches over two threads of fabric unless otherwise specified on the key. Stitch the face and hands using one ply of floss over one thread.

## Striped Ornament Jar

**Supplies**

*10" square of 14-count gold-and-white Aida cloth*
*Cotton embroidery floss*
*DMC metallic floss*
*Purchased 89 mm round brass trinket jar*

**Stitches**

Center and stitch the chart using three plies of floss unless otherwise specified. Press from the back.

**Assembly**

Follow the directions included with the trinket jar.

## Poinsettia Wreath

**Supplies**

*15" square of 28-count cream-and-gold Quaker cloth*
*Cotton embroidery floss*
*Kreinik blending filament*
*Mill Hill bugle beads*
*¼ yard of 45"-wide green velveteen*
*½ yard of 45"-wide red faille or taffeta*
*Tracing paper*
*Erasable fabric marker*
*Matching sewing thread*
*⅞ yard of ⅛"-diameter cording*
*Polyester fiberfill*
*1⅛"-diameter button cover form*

**Stitches**

Center and stitch the chart using three plies of floss unless otherwise specified. Press from the back.

**Assembly**

Draw a 9½"-diameter circle on the tracing paper; cut out. Center the paper pattern on the stitched piece and trace around it with the erasable marker. Cut out on traced line. Use the paper pattern to cut a back from red fabric. Also from red fabric, cut two 3½×40" back ruffle strips and enough 1¼"-wide bias strips to make 30" of piping. From the green velveteen, cut two 2¾×40" ruffle strips. Measurements include ½" seam allowances. Sew seams with right sides together unless otherwise specified in the instructions.

Sew together the short ends of bias strips to make one long piece. Center the cording lengthwise on the wrong side of the bias strip. Fold the fabric around the cording, bringing the raw edges together. Using a zipper foot, sew close to the cording through both layers. Baste the piping to the right side of the stitched piece, overlapping the ends at the center bottom.

Sew the short ends of the 2¾"-wide green ruffle strips together, forming one long strip. Repeat with the 3½"-wide red ruffle strips. Using a ¼" seam allowance, sew the red and green ruffle strips together along one

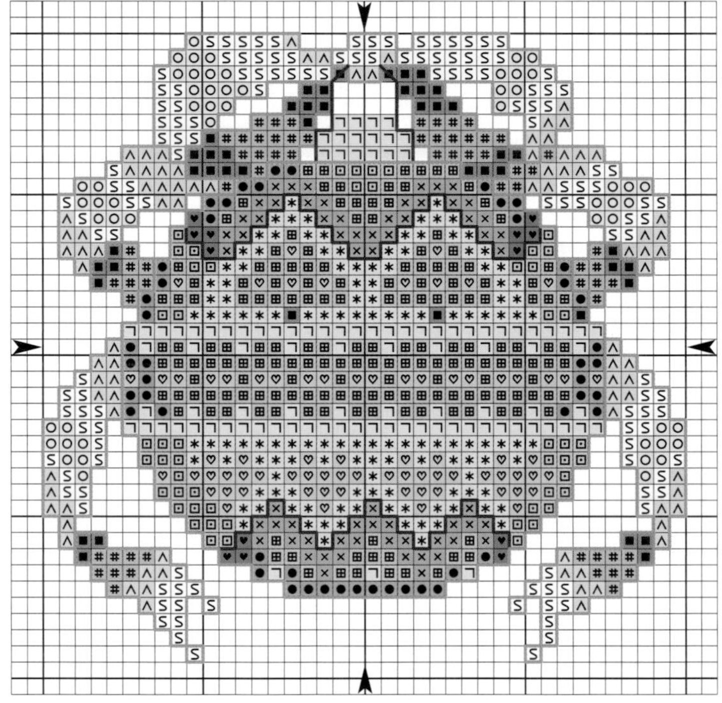

### *Striped Ornament Jar*

| Anchor | Symbol | DMC |
|---|---|---|
| 1025 | × | 347 Salmon |
| 358 | ■ | 433 Dark chestnut |
| 1046 | # | 435 Light chestnut |
| 923 | ● | 699 Dark Christmas green |
| 228 | ⊞ | 700 Medium Christmas green |
| 305 | S | 725 True topaz |
| 293 | O | 727 Pale topaz |
| 307 | ∧ | 783 Christmas gold |
| 1005 | ♥ | 816 Garnet |
| 257 | ⊡ | 905 Dark parrot green |
| 256 | ✱ | 906 Medium parrot green |
| 035 | ♡ | 3705 Watermelon |
|  | ⌉ | 5282 Metallic gold |

BACKSTITCH (1X)
1046 ⁄ 435 Light chestnut – all other stitches
⁄ 5282 Metallic gold – bow, ornament outline

***Ball with Gold Bow Stitch count:*** *39 high x 40 wide*

***Finished design sizes:***
*14-count fabric – 2¾ x 2¾ inches*
*16-count fabric – 2⅜ x 2½ inches*
*18-count fabric – 2⅛ x 2⅛ inches*

long edge. Press the seam allowance toward the red fabric.

Sew the short ends of the ruffle strip together to form a continuous circle. Fold the strip in half lengthwise with wrong sides together; press. Sew two rows of gathering stitches through both layers ½" and ¼" from the raw edge. Pull the stitches to fit the circumference of the pillow front; adjust the gathers evenly. With the green velveteen side next to the pillow front, sew the ruffle along the piping basting line.

Sew the pillow front and back together with right sides facing, leaving an opening for turning. Trim the seams and turn right side out. Press the pillow carefully. Stuff the pillow firmly with fiberfill; slip-stitch the opening closed.

Use green velveteen to cover the button form following the manufacturer's instructions. Using six plies of green floss, insert a long needle into the center of the pillow front. Push the needle through the pillow, exiting at the center of the pillow back. Return the needle to the pillow front. Tighten the thread to make a slight indentation and tie off. Slip the covered button onto the needle. Sew through the pillow several times and secure the thread on the pillow back.

## *Poinsettia Wreath*

| Anchor | | DMC |
|---|---|---|
| 9046 | ◻ | 321 True Christmas red |
| 1005 | ✱ | 498 Dark Christmas red |
| 033 | − | 892 Carnation |
| 897 | ▼ | 902 Garnet |
| 257 | ✕ | 905 Parrot green |
| 246 | ● | 986 Forest green |
| 035 | ○ | 3801 Watermelon |
| 306 | ⧅ | 3820 Straw |
| BACKSTITCH (1X) | | |
| 256 | / | 704 Chartreuse – leaf veins |
| 906 | / | 829 Bronze – berries |
| 380 | / | 838 Beige-brown – all other stitches |
| | / | 5282 Metallic gold |
| FRENCH KNOT (1X wrapped once) | | |
| 380 | ● | 838 Beige-brown – berries |
| MILL HILL BEADS | | |
| | / | 72011 Victorian gold small bugle beads |

***Stitch count:*** *86 high x 86 wide*

***Finished design sizes:***
*28-count fabric – 6¼ x 6¼ inches*
*32-count fabric – 5⅜ x 5⅜ inches*
*20-count fabric – 8¾ x 8¾ inches*

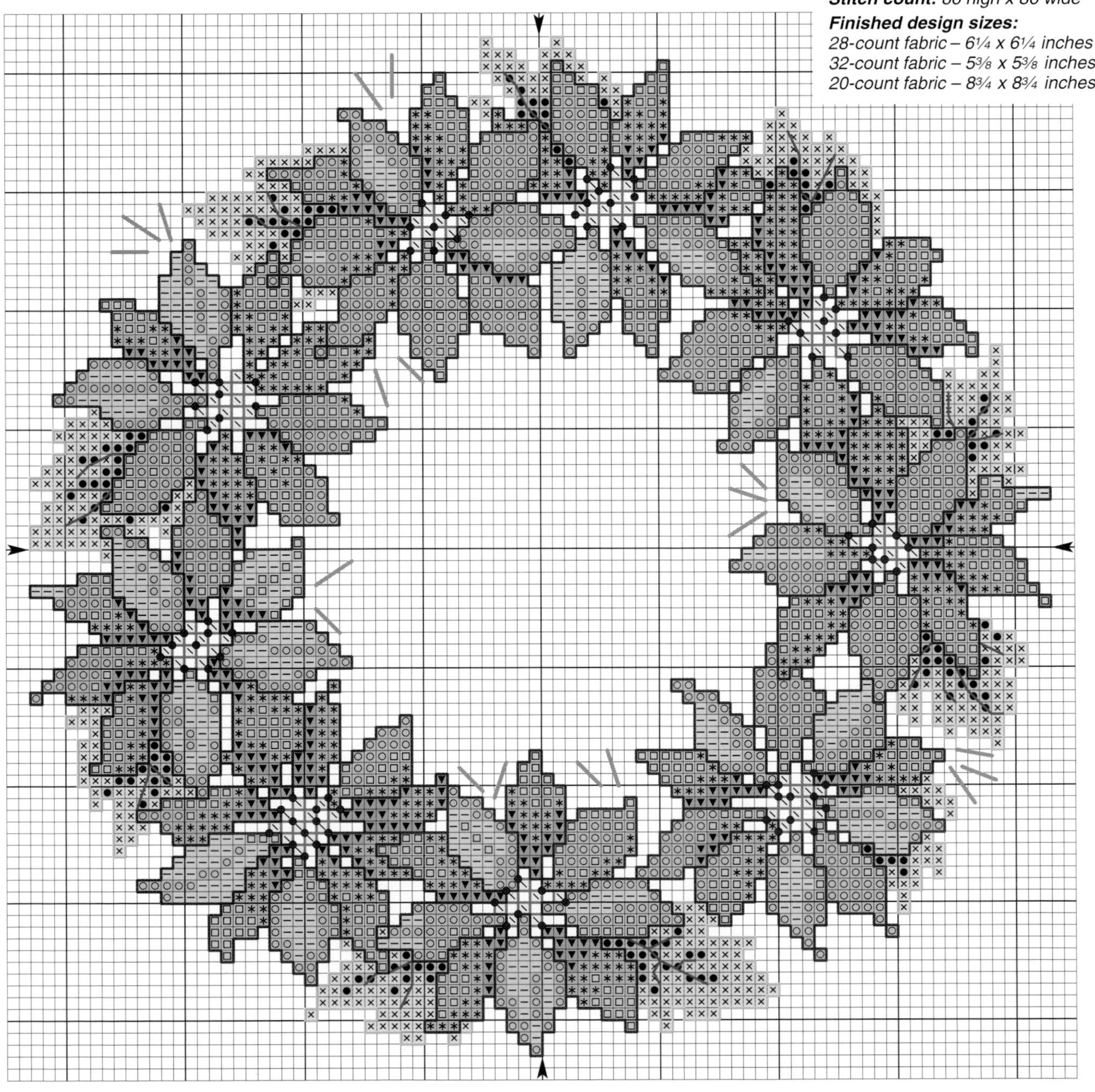

## Partridge Wreath

### Supplies

*13" square of 28-count Christmas red Jubilee fabric*
*Cotton embroidery floss*
*Kreinik blending filament*
*11⅝" crown plate frame*
*100- and 150-grit sandpaper*
*1" flat paint brush*
*Old toothbrush or spatter brush*
*Jo Sonya's Artist's Colors in Napthol red, Rich gold, and Burnt umber*
*10" square of fleece*
*Spray adhesive*

### Stitches

Center and stitch the chart using three plies of floss over two threads of fabric unless otherwise specified.

### Assembly

Remove the mounting board from the frame; set aside. Sand all wooden surfaces of the frame with 100- and then 150-grit sandpaper. Remove the dust with a damp paper towel.

Use a 1" brush to base-coat the frame with Napthol red. Rinse the brush, and allow the paint to dry. Dip the 1" brush in Rich gold; then stroke it on paper toweling several times to remove most of the paint. Brush a thin coat over the frame; allow to dry. Thin a small amount of Burnt umber to the consistency of ink. Use the toothbrush or spatter brush to lightly spatter the paint over the frame; allow to dry.

Use the mounting board as a pattern to cut a circle of fleece. Spray the mounting board lightly with adhesive and press the fleece onto it. Center and smooth the stitched piece on the fleece. Turn the excess fabric to the back and glue. Insert the mounting board into the frame.

*French Knot*

## *Partridge Wreath*

| Anchor | DMC |
|---|---|
| 352 | 300 Deep mahogany |
| 403 | 310 Black |
| 1047 | 402 Pale mahogany |
| 280 | 581 Moss green |
| 046 | 666 Red |
| 891 | 676 Light old gold |
| 901 | 680 Dark old gold |
| 226 | 702 Christmas green |
| 926 | 712 Cream |
| 300 | 745 Yellow |
| 308 | 782 Medium topaz |
| 359 | 801 Coffee brown |
| 230 | 909 Dark emerald |
| 209 | 912 Light emerald |
| 1048 | 3776 Light mahogany |
| 899 | 3782 Mocha |
| 393 | 3790 Beige-gray |
| BLENDED NEEDLE | |
| 300 | 745 Yellow (2X) and 021 Kreinik Copper filament (1X) |
| 295 | 726 Light topaz (2X) and 021 Kreinik Copper filament (1X) |
| BACKSTITCH (1X) | |
| 352 | 300 Deep mahogany - eye |
| 403 | 310 Black - pears, partridge and berries |
| 279 | 734 Olive - pear leaf veins |
| 218 | 890 Pistachio - pear leaves |
| | 5282 Metallic gold - holly leaves |
| STRAIGHT STITCH (1X) | |
| 352 | 300 Deep mahogany - stems |
| 1048 | 3776 Light mahogany - partridge |
| FRENCH KNOT (1X wrapped twice) | |
| 352 | 300 Deep mahogany - ends of pear stems |
| 926 | 712 Cream - eye |

***Stitch count:*** *94 high x 86 wide*

***Finished design sizes:***
*28-count fabric – 6⅝ x 6⅛ inches*
*32-count fabric – 5⅞ x 5⅓ inches*
*36-count fabric – 5¼ x 4¾ inches*

## Merry Christmas

*The chart is on pages 24–25 and the key is below.*

### Supplies

*22×26" piece of 14-count colonial blue Aida cloth*
*Cotton embroidery floss*
*2—additional skeins each of light old gold (DMC 676), pale old gold (677), medium old gold (729), charcoal (3799), and true terra-cotta (3830)*
*Mill Hill seed beads*
*Desired frame*

### Stitches

Center and stitch the chart on the fabric. Use three plies over two threads of fabric unless otherwise specified. Press from the back.

## *Merry Christmas*

| Anchor | DMC |
|---|---|
| 002 | 000 White |
| 978 | 322 Navy |
| 038 | 335 Rose |
| 401 | 413 Pewter |
| 398 | 415 Pearl gray |
| 374 | 420 Medium hazel |
| 373 | 422 Light hazel |
| 1046 | 435 Light chestnut |
| 877 | 502 Blue-green |
| 212 | 561 Dark seafoam |
| 210 | 562 Medium seafoam |
| 891 | 676 Light old gold |
| 886 | 677 Pale old gold |
| 228 | 700 Medium Christmas green |
| 226 | 702 Light Christmas green |
| 295 | 726 Topaz |
| 890 | 729 Medium old gold |
| 303 | 742 Tangerine |
| 1022 | 760 True salmon |
| 359 | 801 Coffee brown |
| 043 | 815 Garnet |
| 271 | 819 Pink |
| 164 | 824 Bright blue |
| 1010 | 951 Ivory |
| 076 | 961 Dark rose-pink |
| 073 | 963 Pale rose-pink |
| 355 | 975 Deep golden brown |
| 1002 | 977 Light golden brown |
| 246 | 986 Forest green |
| 871 | 3041 Medium antique violet |
| 887 | 3046 Yellow-beige |
| 1024 | 3328 Dark salmon |
| 059 | 3350 Dusty rose |
| 1023 | 3712 Medium salmon |
| 896 | 3721 Shell pink |
| 872 | 3740 Dark antique violet |
| 1013 | 3778 Terra-cotta |
| 363 | 3827 Pale golden brown |
| 901 | 3829 Deep old gold |
| 5975 | 3830 True terra-cotta |
| BACKSTITCH | |
| 358 | 433 Dark chestnut – bird's wing and tail, basket detail (1X) |
| 043 | 815 Garnet – candy, berry detail (1X) |
| 164 | 824 Bright blue – basket ribbon (1X) |
| 1044 | 895 Hunter green – basket ribbon, jar topper, and leaf veins (1X) |
| 236 | 3799 Charcoal – package print, corner pattern (1X) |
| 236 | 3799 Charcoal – all other stitches (2X) |
| LAZY DAISY (1X) | |
| 382 | 3371 Black-brown – inner design of circle on "Merry Christmas" banner, diagonal strip in lower right corner |
| FRENCH KNOT (1X wrapped twice) | |
| 236 | 3799 Charcoal – detail on packages, detail on circular border around "C", corner detail and berries |
| MILL HILL BEADS | |
| | 00128 Dark yellow seed beads |
| | 00145 Pink seed beads |
| | 00165 Christmas red seed beads |
| | 00167 Christmas green seed beads |
| | 02014 Black seed beads |

***Stitch count:*** *186 high x 135 wide*

***Finished design sizes:***
*14-count fabric – 13¼ x 9⅝ inches*
*16-count fabric – 11⅝ x 8⅜ inches*
*18-count fabric – 10⅓ x 7½ inches*

## Apple Ornament

*The chart and key are on page 26.*

### Supplies

*9" square of 28-count raw linen*
*Cotton embroidery floss*
*4¼"-diameter circle of self-stick mounting board with foam*
*½ yard of ⅜"-wide metallic gold-and-red trim*
*6" length of ⅛"-wide metallic braid*
*Crafts glue*
*4" circle of beige felt*

### Stitches

Center and stitch the chart using three plies of floss over two threads of fabric unless otherwise specified. Press from the back.

*Continued*

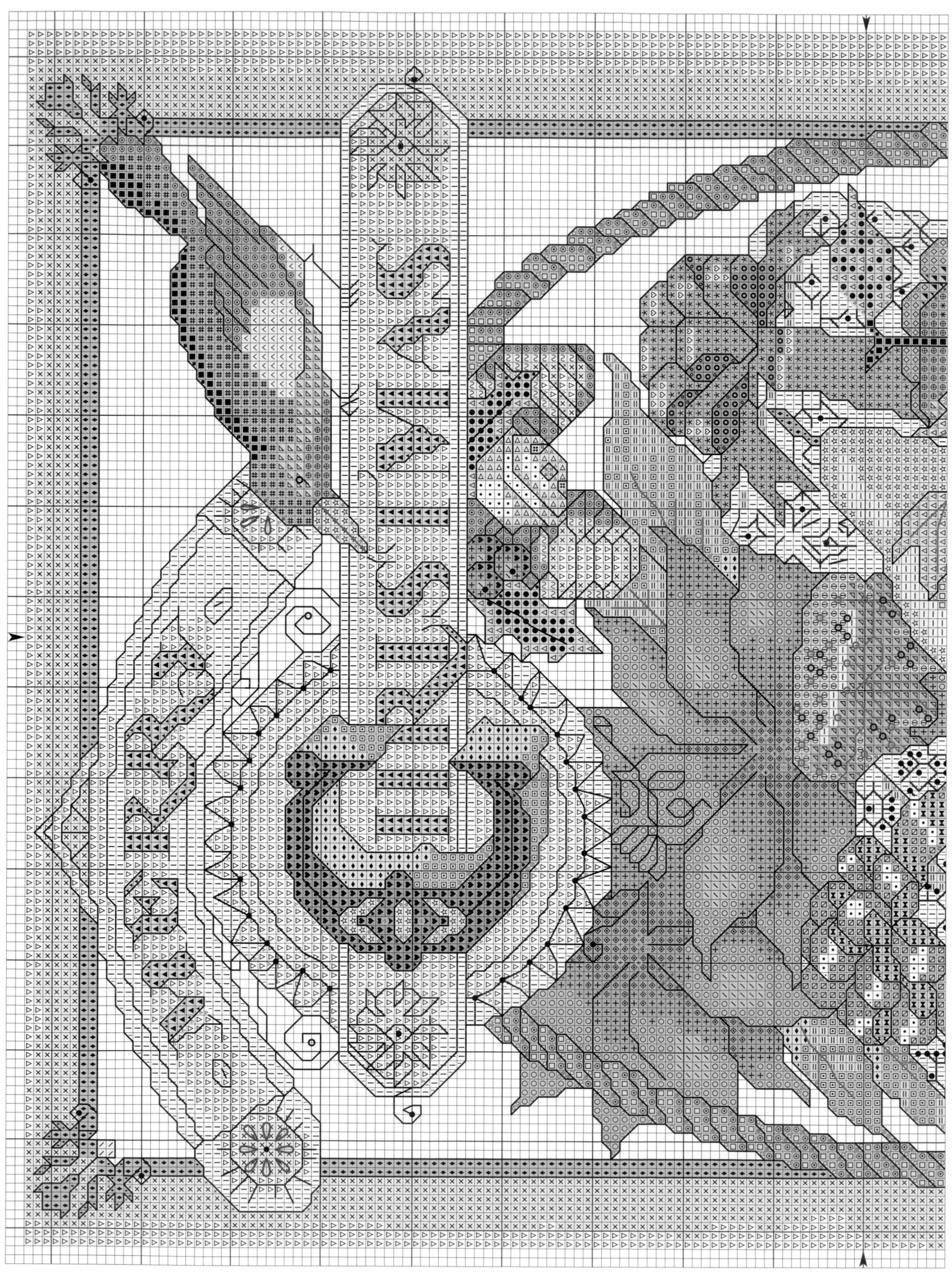

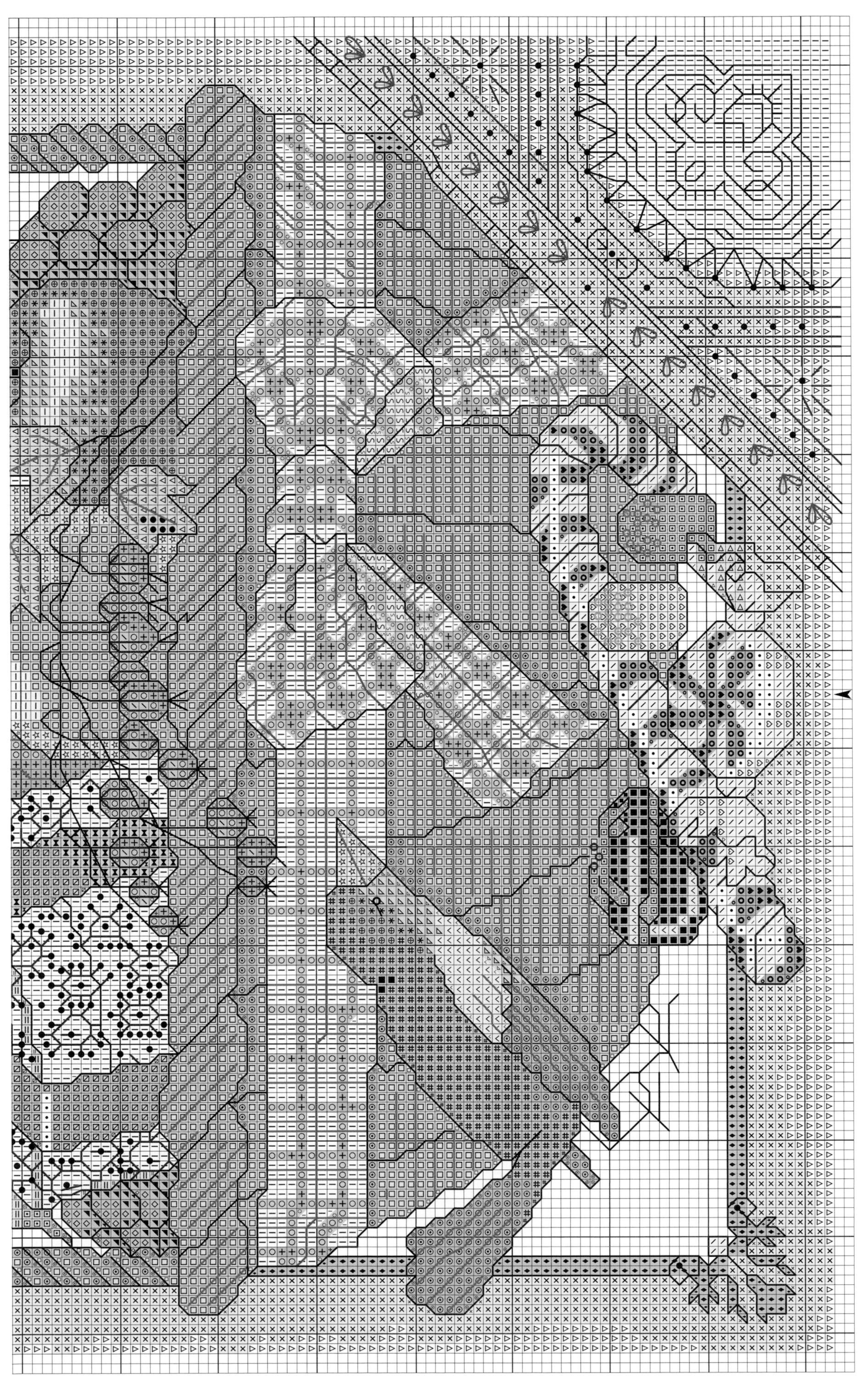

## *Apple Ornament*

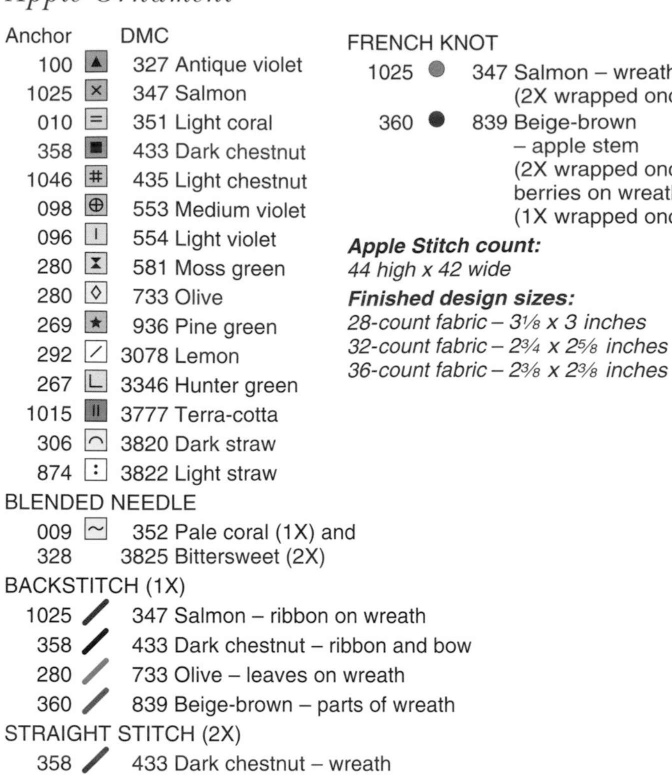

| Anchor | | DMC |
|---|---|---|
| 100 | ▲ | 327 Antique violet |
| 1025 | × | 347 Salmon |
| 010 | = | 351 Light coral |
| 358 | ■ | 433 Dark chestnut |
| 1046 | # | 435 Light chestnut |
| 098 | ⊕ | 553 Medium violet |
| 096 | I | 554 Light violet |
| 280 | ⧗ | 581 Moss green |
| 280 | ◊ | 733 Olive |
| 269 | ★ | 936 Pine green |
| 292 | ⁄ | 3078 Lemon |
| 267 | L | 3346 Hunter green |
| 1015 | ‖ | 3777 Terra-cotta |
| 306 | ⌒ | 3820 Dark straw |
| 874 | : | 3822 Light straw |

BLENDED NEEDLE

| | | |
|---|---|---|
| 009 | ~ | 352 Pale coral (1X) and |
| 328 | | 3825 Bittersweet (2X) |

BACKSTITCH (1X)

| | | |
|---|---|---|
| 1025 | / | 347 Salmon – ribbon on wreath |
| 358 | / | 433 Dark chestnut – ribbon and bow |
| 280 | / | 733 Olive – leaves on wreath |
| 360 | / | 839 Beige-brown – parts of wreath |

STRAIGHT STITCH (2X)

| | | |
|---|---|---|
| 358 | / | 433 Dark chestnut – wreath |

FRENCH KNOT

| | | |
|---|---|---|
| 1025 | ● | 347 Salmon – wreath (2X wrapped once) |
| 360 | ● | 839 Beige-brown – apple stem (2X wrapped once), berries on wreath (1X wrapped once) |

***Apple Stitch count:***
*44 high x 42 wide*

***Finished design sizes:***
*28-count fabric – 3⅛ x 3 inches*
*32-count fabric – 2¾ x 2⅝ inches*
*36-count fabric – 2⅜ x 2⅜ inches*

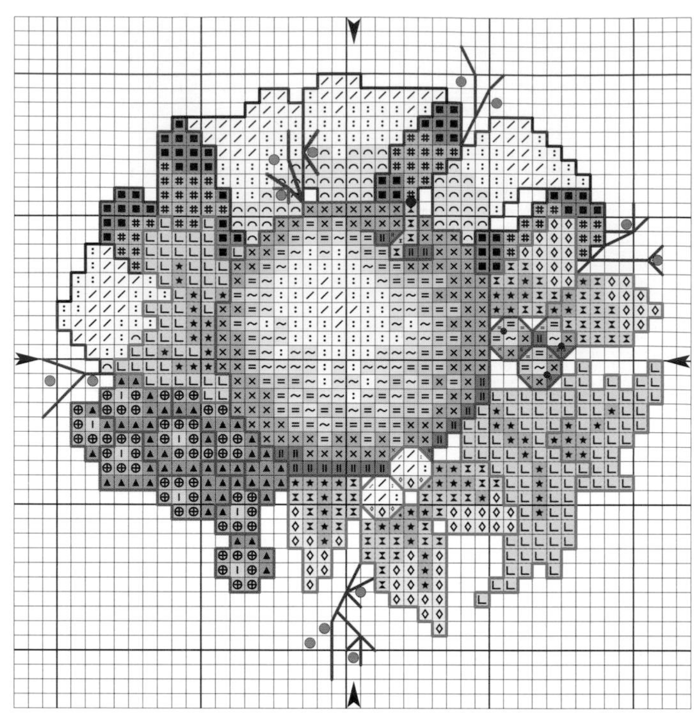

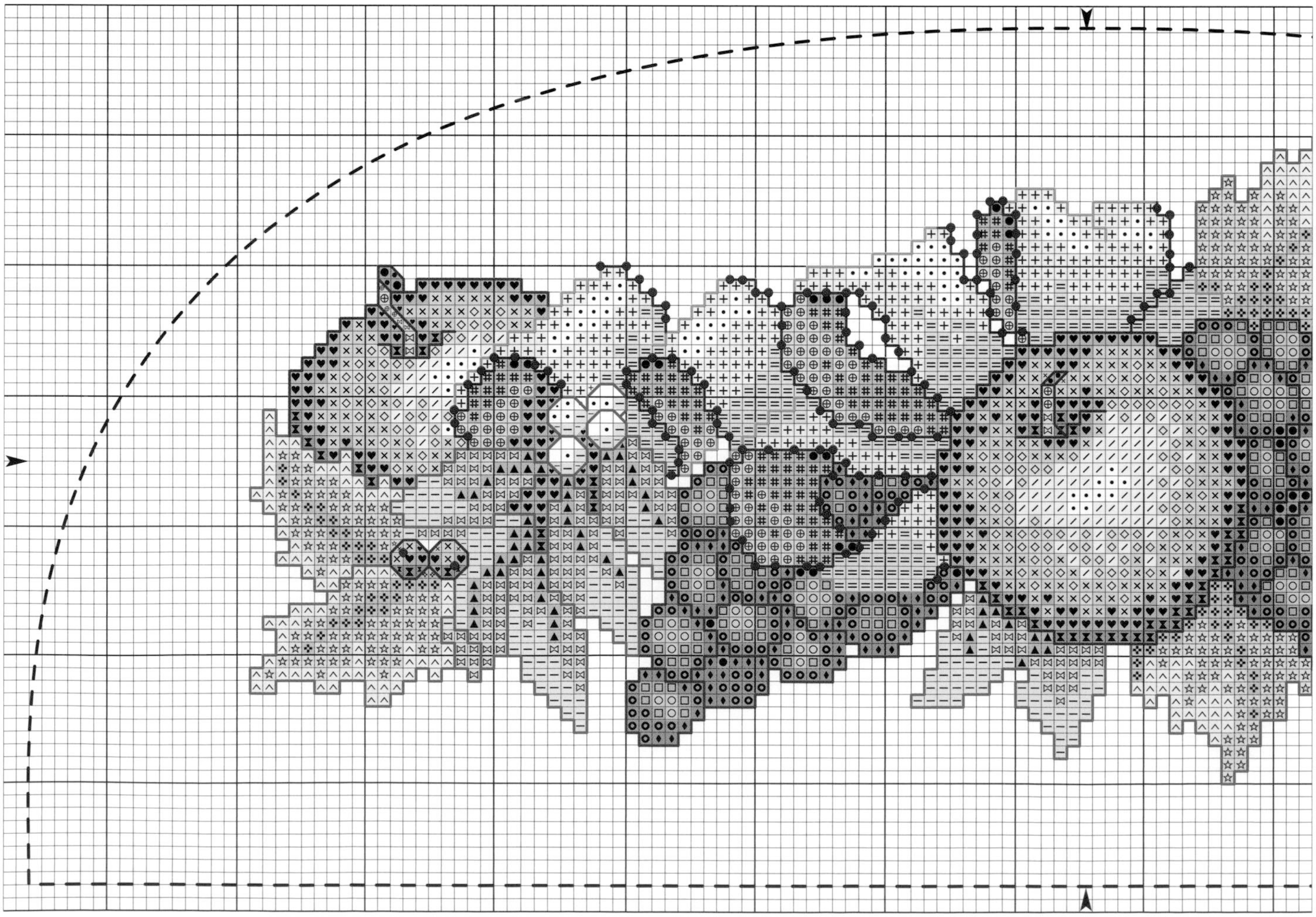

**Assembly**

Peel the protective paper from the mounting board. Center the foam side on the back of the stitchery and press to stick. Trim the excess fabric ½" beyond the edge of the board. Fold the excess fabric to the back and glue in place.

Position and glue the metallic trim around the edge of the ornament, overlapping the ends at the bottom center and trimming the excess.

For the hanger, fold the braid in half to form a loop. Glue the braid ends to the top center of the ornament back. Glue the felt to the back of the ornament.

## Fruit, Holly, and Mistletoe Arch

**Supplies**

*14×22" piece of 22-count ivory Janina fabric*
*Cotton embroidery floss*
*Erasable fabric marker*
*Tracing paper*
*9×18" piece of self-stick mounting board with foam*
*⅝ yard of ½"-wide red flat braid trim*
*7×16" piece of cream felt*
*Crafts glue*

**Stitches**

Center and stitch the chart using four plies of floss over two threads of fabric unless otherwise specified. Press from the back.

**Assembly**

Use the erasable marker to draw an outline around the stitched area of the design as indicated by the dashed line on the chart; *do not* cut out. Place the tracing paper over the fabric and trace the arch outline. Cut out the paper pattern. Use the paper pattern to cut matching shapes from the mounting board and the felt.

Peel the protective paper from the mounting board. Center the foam side on the back of the stitchery and press to stick. Trim the excess fabric 1" beyond the edge of the board. Fold the excess fabric to the back and glue in place.

Position and glue the trim around the edge of the arch. Fold the trim ends to the back and glue. Glue the felt to the back of the arch.

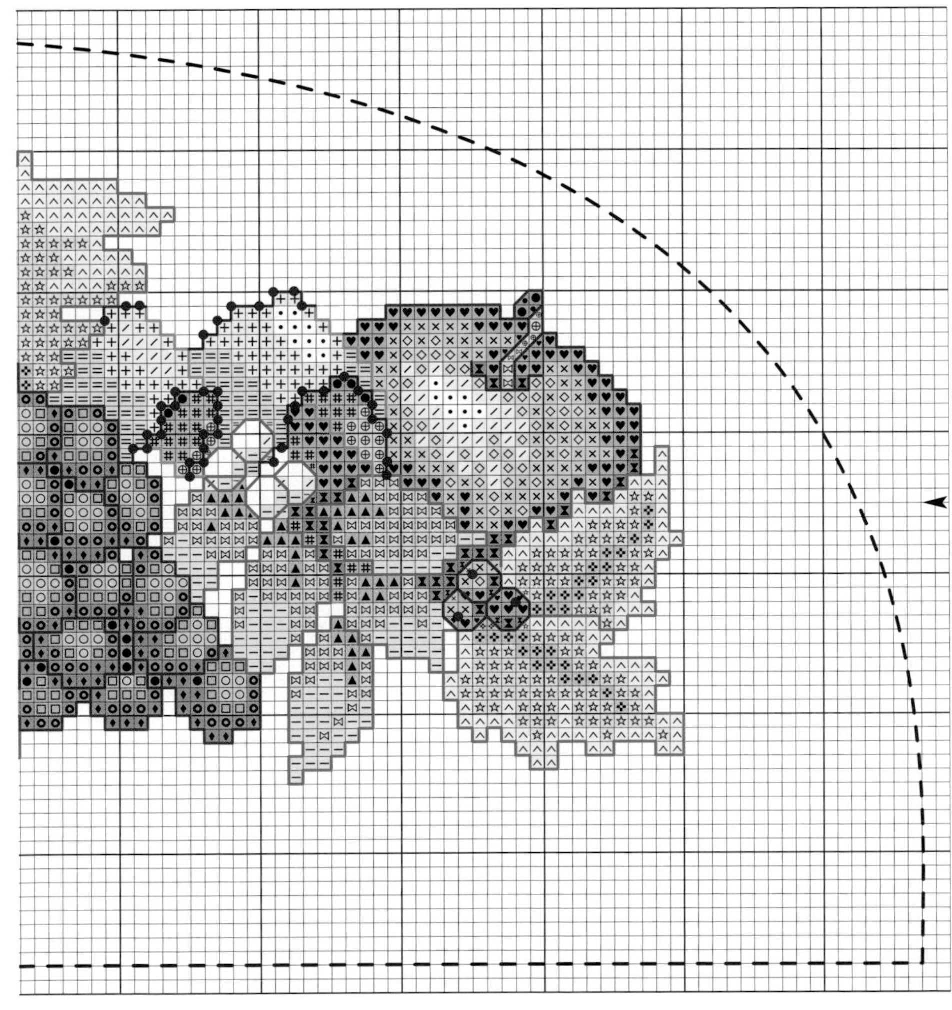

### *Fruit, Holly, and Mistletoe Arch*

| Anchor | | DMC |
|---|---|---|
| 100 | ◙ | 327 Antique violet |
| 1025 | ♥ | 347 Salmon |
| 010 | ☒ | 351 Light coral |
| 310 | # | 434 Chestnut |
| 267 | ☆ | 470 Avocado |
| 102 | ♦ | 550 Deep violet |
| 098 | ▣ | 553 Medium violet |
| 305 | + | 725 True topaz |
| 845 | ▲ | 730 Dark olive |
| 281 | ⋈ | 732 True olive |
| 279 | − | 734 Pale olive |
| 309 | ⊕ | 781 Dark topaz |
| 307 | = | 783 Christmas gold |
| 268 | ✣ | 937 Pine green |
| 360 | ● | 3031 Mocha |
| 292 | • | 3078 Lemon |
| 1016 | ○ | 3727 Antique mauve |
| 1015 | ⧗ | 3777 Terra-cotta |
| 278 | ^ | 3819 Moss green |
| 874 | / | 3822 Straw |
| BLENDED NEEDLE | | |
| 328 | ◇ | 3825 Bittersweet (2X) and |
| 009 | | 352 Pale coral (1X) |
| BACKSTITCH (1X) | | |
| 845 | / | 730 Dark olive – leaves and mistletoe berries |
| 309 | / | 781 Dark topaz – ribbon |
| 359 | / | 801 Coffee brown – fruit and holly berries |
| 089 | / | 917 Plum – ribbon edge |
| FRENCH KNOT (1X wrapped once) | | |
| 359 | ● | 801 Coffee brown – holly berries |
| 089 | ● | 917 Plum – ribbon edge |

***Stitch count:*** *50 high x 129 wide*

***Finished design sizes:***
*22-count fabric – 4½ x 11¾ inches*
*25-count fabric – 4 x 10⅜ inches*
*28-count fabric – 3½ x 9¼ inches*

# Homespun

# Holidays

*Even if you live in the heart of the city, and cutting a tree in the woods, loading it onto a sled, and pulling it home on a snowy afternoon is but a dream, you can still cross-stitch the warm feelings of a country Christmas.*

Simplicity is the key to homespun country decor. This old-time feather tree adorned with candles, *above,* is trimmed on the bias and outlined with piping to accent the tree's angular shape.

Give the kitchen a folk-art holiday look, *opposite.* Mix and match the six motifs with color coordinated banding and fabrics to adorn towels, hot pads, mug mats, and containers for holiday treats.

*Designs: Ornament, Barbara Sestok; folk-art kitchen items, De Selby*

If you want a country-style tree, stitch some rustic ornaments to hang from the branches. You'll want to make several traditional country houses, *opposite,* stitched in subtle colors on 35-count natural linen and embellished with twisted cord.

Simple straight stitches anchor the quilt sashing as well as the folksy star that surrounds the country cottage, *below.* Trim your with an old-fashioned braided floss hanger.

*Designs: House, Drawn Thread; star, Bent Creek*

Dress for the season in a vest that's both easy to stitch and comfortable, *opposite*. Keep your fingers warm in cozy mittens embellished with tree and heart motifs, *right*.

The whimsical sampler, *below*, features a colorful sheep button, and can be worked two ways. Stitch it on Aida cloth and finish it into a simple treat bag. Or, work it on linen, complete with hemstitched edges and ribbons to gather the ends of a nifty needle roll.

*Designs: Vest and mittens, De Selby; ornaments, Shepherd's Bush*

Many Christmas memories, like photographs and greeting cards, appear on paper. When you store those special treasures together in an heirloom album, you can review and relive the good times again and again. This touching album cover fits a standard loose-leaf notebook to accommodate your own unique mementos.

*Design: Gail Bussi*

## Feather Tree Ornament

### Supplies

*10" square of 14-count Linaida cloth*
*1/4 yard of 45"-wide green-and-black check cotton fabric*
*4" square of thick batting*
*Cotton embroidery floss*
*DMC metallic embroidery floss*
*Mill Hill seed beads*
*1/2 yard of 1/8"-diameter cording*
*20" piece of jute string*
*Matching sewing thread*

### Stitches

Center and stitch the chart using two plies of floss unless otherwise specified. Press from the back.

### Assembly

Centering the design, trim the finished stitchery into a 4½" diamond. From the green-and-black check fabric, cut one 4½"-square back and a 1¼×18" bias strip for piping. All measurements include a ¼" seam allowance.

For the piping, center the cording lengthwise on the wrong side of the bias strip. Fold the fabric around the cording with the raw edges together. Using a zipper foot, sew close to the cording through both fabric layers. Baste the piping to the right side of the stitchery, overlapping the ends at the bottom of the stitchery.

For the hanger, fold a 7" length of jute in half. Sew the jute to the top center of the ornament front, aligning the jute ends with the raw edges.

Sew the ornament front to the back with right sides facing and leaving an opening for turning. Clip the corners, and turn right side out. Insert the batting in opening. Hand-sew the opening closed. Tie a bow around the base of the hanger with the remaining jute; trim the excess jute.

## Folk-Art Kitchen Towel

*The chart and key are on page 38.*

### Supplies

*3/4 yard of 27-count 6"-wide green-and-white Checkers linen banding*
*Cotton embroidery floss*
*Purchased 18×27" hand towel*
*Matching sewing thread*

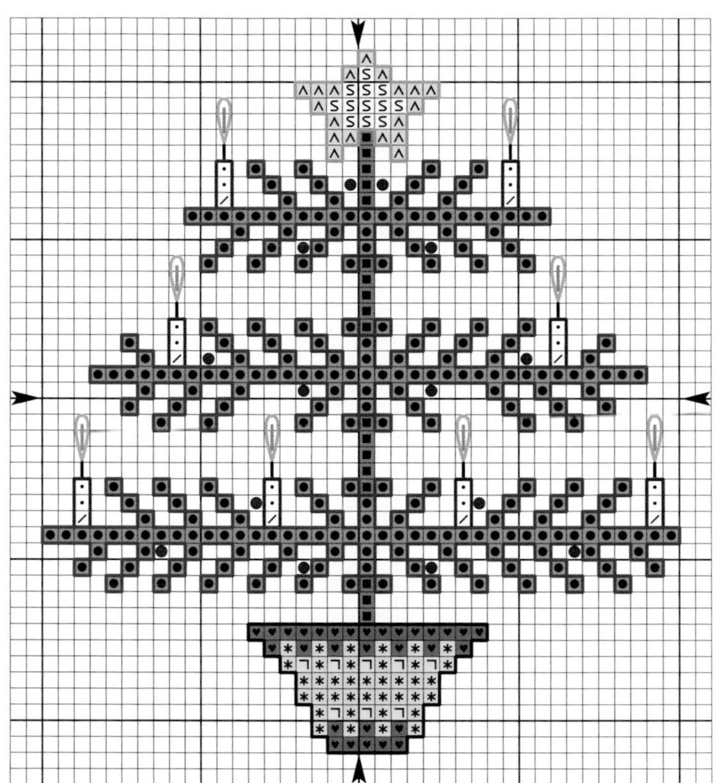

### Stitches

Center and stitch the chart so the bottom row of stitches is 3" from one end of the banding. Use three plies of floss over two threads of fabric unless otherwise specified.

### Assembly

Press under ¼" on the end of the banding closest to the stitching. Center the banding lengthwise on the towel, aligning the pressed edge with the end of the towel. Topstitch the banding to the towel, trimming and turning under the unstitched end of the banding.

## Cinnamon Stick Jar

*The chart and key are on page 38.*

### Supplies

*12 to 15" of 27-count 3⅞"-wide green-and-white Country Aire linen banding*
*Cotton embroidery floss*
*1/4 to 3/8"-diameter buttons*
*Short jar or drinking glass*
*1 yard of 1/8"-wide ribbon*

### Stitches

Center and stitch one motif on the banding using two plies of floss over two threads of fabric unless otherwise specified. Stitch additional motifs to

*Continued*

### *Feather Tree Ornament*

| Anchor | | DMC |
|---|---|---|
| 358 | ■ | 433 Dark chestnut |
| 923 | ● | 699 Dark Christmas green |
| 305 | S | 725 True topaz |
| 275 | • | 746 Off-white |
| 307 | ^ | 783 Christmas gold |
| 1005 | ♥ | 816 Garnet |
| 256 | ✱ | 906 Medium parrot green |
| 292 | / | 3078 Lemon |
| | ┐ | 5282 Metallic gold |

BACKSTITCH (1X)

| | | |
|---|---|---|
| 358 | / | 433 Dark chestnut – candle wicks, base of tree |
| 1046 | / | 435 Light chestnut – candles |
| 255 | / | 907 Light parrot green – tree |
| | / | 5282 Metallic gold – star |

STRAIGHT STITCH (2X)

| | | |
|---|---|---|
| 329 | / | 3340 Melon – center of candle flames |

MILL HILL BEADS

● 00968 Red seed beads – feather tree

LAZY DAISY (2X)

5282 Metallic gold – candle flames

***Tree with Candles Stitch count:***
*44 high x 40 wide*
***Finished design sizes:***
*14-count fabric – 3⅛ x 2¾ inches*
*16-count fabric – 2¾ x 2½ inches*
*18-count fabric – 2⅜ x 2⅛ inches*

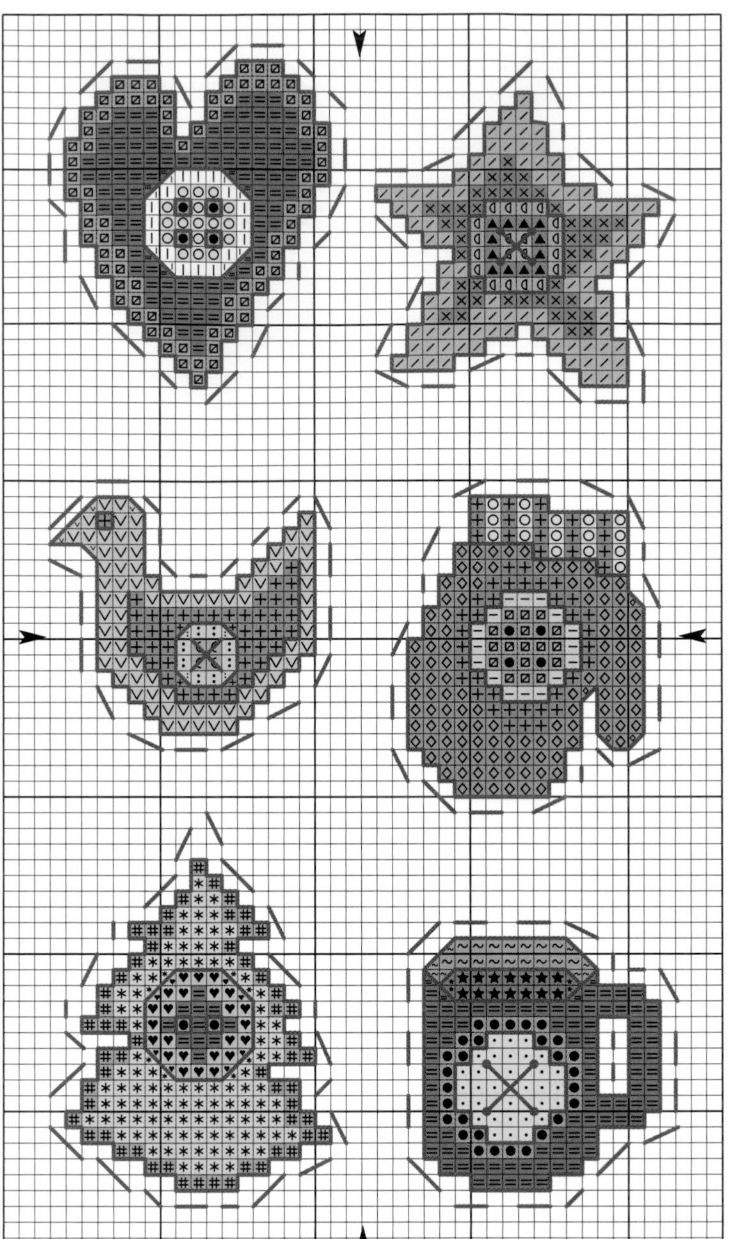

*Folk-Art Accessories*

| Anchor | | DMC | |
|---|---|---|---|
| 9046 | ♥ | 321 | Christmas red |
| 1025 | ▬ | 347 | Deep salmon |
| 5975 | ◇ | 356 | Medium terra-cotta |
| 275 | · | 746 | Off-white |
| 1022 | ~ | 760 | True salmon |
| 1021 | ☾ | 761 | Light salmon |
| 127 | + | 823 | Navy |
| 164 | ▲ | 824 | Deep bright blue |
| 161 | ◖ | 826 | Medium bright blue |
| 160 | V | 827 | Powder blue |
| 382 | ● | 3371 | Black-brown |
| 1020 | : | 3713 | Pale salmon |
| 1015 | ★ | 3777 | Deep terra-cotta |
| 188 | ✱ | 3814 | Aquamarine |
| 876 | ⧄ | 3816 | True celadon green |
| 875 | − | 3817 | Light celadon green |
| 306 | # | 3820 | Dark straw |
| 305 | ⁄ | 3821 | True straw |
| 874 | ○ | 3822 | Light straw |
| 386 | I | 3823 | Yellow |
| 340 | ✕ | 3830 | Terra-cotta |

BACKSTITCH

| | | | |
|---|---|---|---|
| 382 | ⁄ | 3371 | Black-brown (1X) |

FRENCH KNOT

| | | | |
|---|---|---|---|
| 382 | • | 3371 | Black-brown (1X wrapped once) |

***Towel***
***Stitch count:*** *74 high x 40 wide*
***Finished design sizes:***
*8-count fabric – 9¼ x 5 inches*
*14-count fabric – 5¼ x 2¾ inches*
*16-count fabric – 4⅝ x 2½ inches*

***Heart***
***Stitch count:*** *23 high x 19 wide*
***Finished design sizes:***
*8-count fabric – 2⅞ x 2⅜ inches*
*14-count fabric – 1⅝ x 1⅜ inches*
*16-count fabric – 1⅜ x 1⅛ inches*

***Star***
***Stitch count:*** *22 high x 19 wide*
***Finished design sizes:***
*8-count fabric – 2¾ x 2⅓ inches*
*14-count fabric – 1½ x 1¼ inches*
*16-count fabric – 1⅜ x 1⅛ inches*

***Bird***
***Stitch count:*** *17 high x 18 wide*
***Finished design sizes:***
*8-count fabric – 2⅛ x 2¼ inches*
*14-count fabric – 1⅛ x 1¼ inches*
*16-count fabric – 1 x 1⅛ inches*

***Mitten***
***Stitch count:*** *21 high x 17 wide*
***Finished design sizes:***
*8-count fabric – 2⅝ x 2⅛ inches*
*14-count fabric – 1½ x 1⅛ inches*
*16-count fabric – 1¼ x 1⅛ inches*

***Tree***
***Stitch count:*** *25 high x 19 wide*
***Finished design sizes:***
*8-count fabric – 3⅛ x 2⅜ inches*
*14-count fabric – 1¾ x 1⅓ inches*
*16-count fabric – 1½ x 1⅛ inches*

***Mug***
***Stitch count:*** *18 high x 17 wide*
***Finished design sizes:***
*8-count fabric – 2¼ x 2⅛ inches*
*14-count fabric – 1¼ x 1⅛ inches*
*16-count fabric – 1⅛ x 1 inches*

the left and right, leaving 16 threads between each one.

**Assembly**

Sew a button to the center of each motif. Thread the ribbon through the eyelets at the top and bottom of the banding. Fold under one short end of the banding. Wrap the banding around the jar, overlapping the folded end. Hand-stitch the ends together.

## Folk-Art Mug Mats

**Supplies**

*For each mat*
*6" square of 8-count white Aida cloth*
*Cotton embroidery floss*
*Erasable fabric marker*
*6" square of green-and-white gingham or other fabric*
*Plastic pellets and/or potpourri*
*¼"-diameter button*

**Stitches**

Center and stitch one motif from the chart using four plies of floss for cross-stitches and two plies for backstitches.

**Assembly**

Use the marker to draw a simplified outline of the motif ½" beyond the running stitch outline. Cut out ¼" beyond the outline. Use the stitched piece to cut a back from the gingham.

With right sides together, sew the stitched piece to the back along the drawn line, leaving a small opening for turning. Clip seam allowances and turn right side out. Pour potpourri and plastic pellets into the opening. Hand-stitch the opening closed. Sew the button in the middle of the design, stitching through all layers.

## Folk-Art Hot Pads

**Supplies**

*For each hot pad*
*8" square of 14-count white Aida cloth*
*Cotton embroidery floss*
*6½" square of green-and-white gingham or other fabric*
*¾ yard of 27-count ⅝"-wide green-and-white Checkers linen ribbon*
*6½" square of batting*
*5 assorted buttons*

**Stitches**

Center and stitch one motif from the chart on the fabric using three plies of floss unless otherwise specified.

**Assembly**

Centering the motif, trim the fabric to a 6½" square. From the gingham, cut a 6½" back and a 2×28" binding strip.

Cut the ribbon into four equal lengths. Topstitch one piece to each side, ½" from the cut edge, and trim the ends even with the edges of the fabric. Layer the back, batting, and stitched piece. Quilt as desired.

Press under ½" on one long edge of the binding strip. Align the remaining long edge with a raw edge on the back of the hot pad. Sew the binding strip around the hot pad using a ½" seam allowance and mitering the corners. Turn the folded edge to the right side and topstitch close to the pressed edge through all layers.

## Holiday House Ornament

**Supplies**

*8" square of 35-count natural brown linen*
*3" square of tan felt*
*Cotton embroidery floss*
*1—additional skein of garnet (DMC 902)*
*3" square of self-stick mounting board with foam*
*Crafts glue*

**Stitches**

Center and stitch the chart using one ply of floss over two threads of fabric unless otherwise specified in the key. Press from the back.

**Assembly**

Peel the protective paper from the mounting board. Center the foam side on the back of the stitchery and press to stick. Trim the excess fabric ½" beyond the edge of the board. Fold the excess fabric to the back and glue in place.

For the twisted cord hanger, cut two 20" lengths of garnet floss (DMC 902). Combine the plies into a single 12-ply strand. Secure one end of the joined strands and twist until tightly wound. Holding the ends, fold the strand in half as the two halves twist around each other. Knot or glue the unfinished end to secure it. Fold the cord in half to form a loop. Glue the cord ends to the top center of the ornament back. Glue the felt to the back of the ornament.

For the twisted cord bow and edging, cut two 66"-long six-ply lengths of garnet floss (DMC 902). Combine the plies and twist as directed *above.*

Find the center of the twisted cord, and tack or glue it to the bottom point of the ornament. Glue the remaining cord around the ornament to the top point. Tie the cord in a bow at the top of the ornament. Tie a knot in each cord end; trim.

*Holiday House Ornament*

| Anchor | | DMC |
|---|---|---|
| 387 | • | Ecru |
| 862 | ♦ | 520 Olive drab |
| 889 | # | 610 Drab brown |
| 830 | ^ | 644 Beige-gray |
| 361 | + | 738 Tan |
| 897 | ♥ | 902 Garnet |
| 851 | O | 924 Deep gray-blue |
| 850 | × | 926 Medium gray-blue |
| 848 | / | 927 Light gray-blue |

***Stitch count:** 60 high x 60 wide*

***Finished design sizes:***
*35-count fabric – 3½ x 3½ inches*
*28-count fabric – 4¼ x 4¼ inches*
*32-count fabric – 3¾ x 3¾ inches*

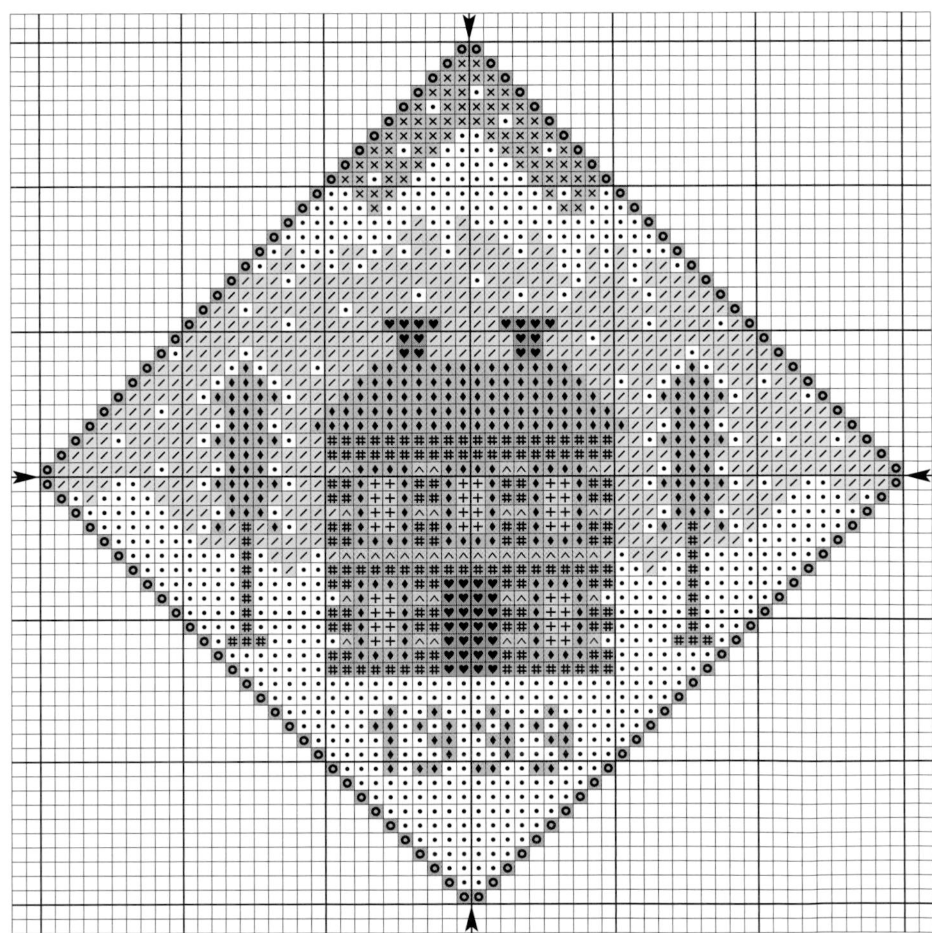

## Cottage Star Ornament

**Supplies**

*12" square of 32-count lambswool linen*
*Cotton embroidery floss*
*¼ yard of 45"-wide plaid cotton fabric*
*7" square of fleece*
*Matching sewing thread*

**Stitches**

Center and stitch the chart on the linen using two plies of floss over two threads unless otherwise specified. Press from the back.

**Assembly**

Centering the design, trim the stitched piece ⅝" beyond the outermost cross-stitches on all four sides. The piece should measure 4½×5".

Cut four 1¼×6¼" sashing strips from the plaid fabric. All measurements include a ¼" seam allowance. Center and sew a sashing strip to the left and right edges of the stitchery with the right sides together and raw edges even. Trim the ends of the strips even with the top and bottom edges of stitchery. Press seam allowances away from the stitched piece. Sew sashing strips to the top and bottom edges in the same manner. Trim the strips even at the sides. Press the seam allowances away from the stitched piece. Thread a needle with two plies of brown-gray floss (DMC 3021). Make random straight stitches across the seam allowances, referring to photograph on *page 33* for placement.

Using the pieced front as a pattern, cut one back from the plaid fabric and one interlining from the fleece.

Baste the fleece to the wrong side of the pieced front. Sew the ornament front and the ornament back together with right sides facing, leaving an opening for turning. Trim the seams, clip the corners, and turn right side out. Hand-sew the opening closed.

For the hanger, cut three six-ply 18" lengths of pine green (DMC 935), deep garnet (DMC 902), and true hazel (DMC 3828) floss. Knot the strands together 1" from one end. Braid until the piece measures 12"; knot. Trim floss 1" beyond the knot. Hand-sew the knots to the top corners of the ornament.

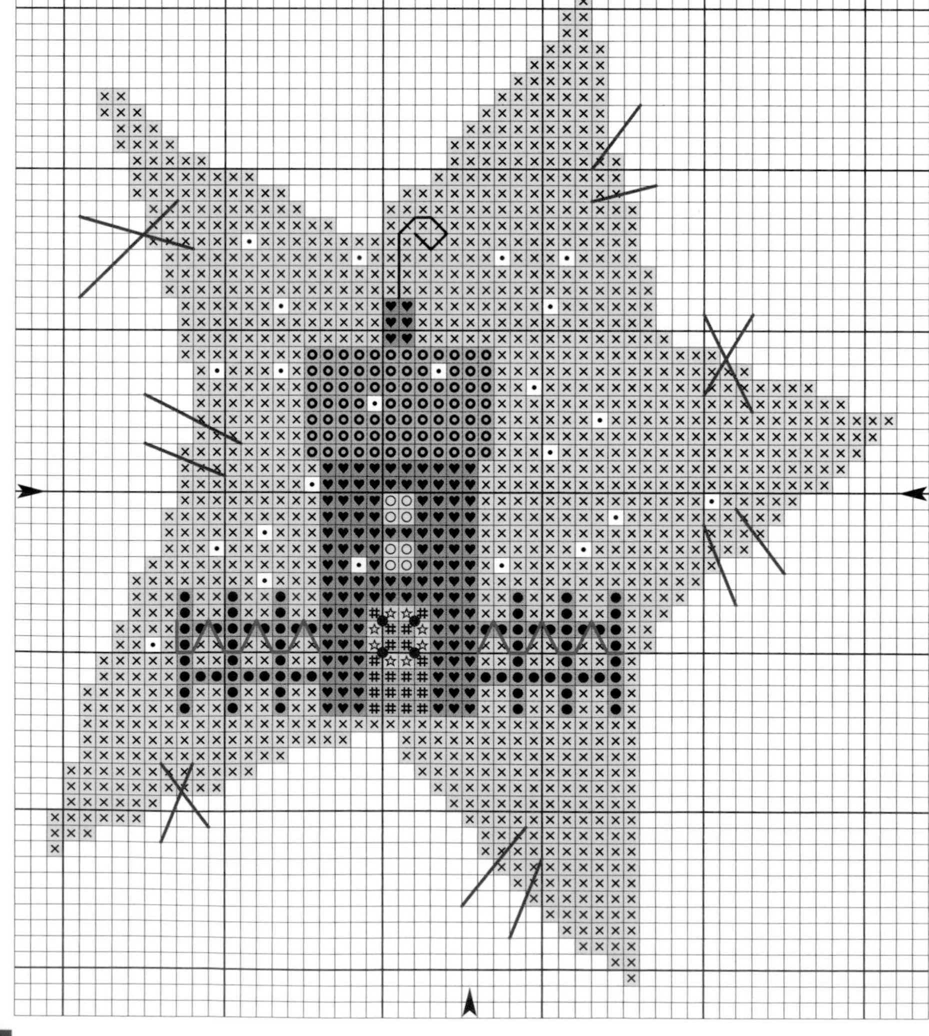

### *Holly Vest*

| Anchor | | DMC |
|---|---|---|
| 218 | ▲ | 319 Dark pistachio |
| 215 | ☒ | 320 True pistachio |
| 9046 | ◇ | 321 True Christmas red |
| 217 | ☆ | 367 Medium pistachio |
| 1005 | ◎ | 498 Dark Christmas red |
| 045 | ♥ | 814 Garnet |
| BACKSTITCH | | |
| 218 | / | 319 Dark pistachio – holly leaves (3X) and vines (4X) |
| 1005 | / | 498 Dark Christmas red – blocks (3X) |
| RAILROAD STITCH | | |
| | + | 032 Watercolors Passion overdyed floss – stripes (2X) |
| FRENCH KNOT | | |
| 1005 | ● | 498 Dark Christmas red – holly berries (6X wrapped once) |

***Stitch count:*** *153 high x 48 wide*

***Finished design sizes:***
*7-count fabric – 21⅞ x 6⅞ inches*
*10-count fabric – 15⅓ x 4⅞ inches*
*14-count fabric – 11 x 3½ inches*

### *Cottage Star Ornament*

| Anchor | | DMC |
|---|---|---|
| 002 | • | 000 White |
| 374 | ○ | 420 Medium hazel |
| 898 | # | 611 Drab brown |
| 1044 | ☆ | 895 Hunter green |
| 897 | ♥ | 902 Deep garnet |
| 861 | ◎ | 935 Pine green |
| 905 | ● | 3021 Brown-gray |
| 373 | ☒ | 3828 True hazel |
| STRAIGHT STITCH | | |
| 1044 | / | 895 Hunter green – garland (4X) |
| 905 | / | 3021 Brown-gray – edge of star (2X) |
| 236 | / | 3799 Charcoal – chimney smoke (2X) |
| FRENCH KNOT | | |
| 045 | ● | 814 Dark garnet – wreath (2X) |

***Stitch count:*** *62 high x 53 wide*

***Finished design sizes:***
*32-count fabric – 3⅞ x 3⅓ inches*
*28-count fabric – 4⅜ x 3¾ inches*
*36-count fabric – 3⅜ x 2⅞ inches*

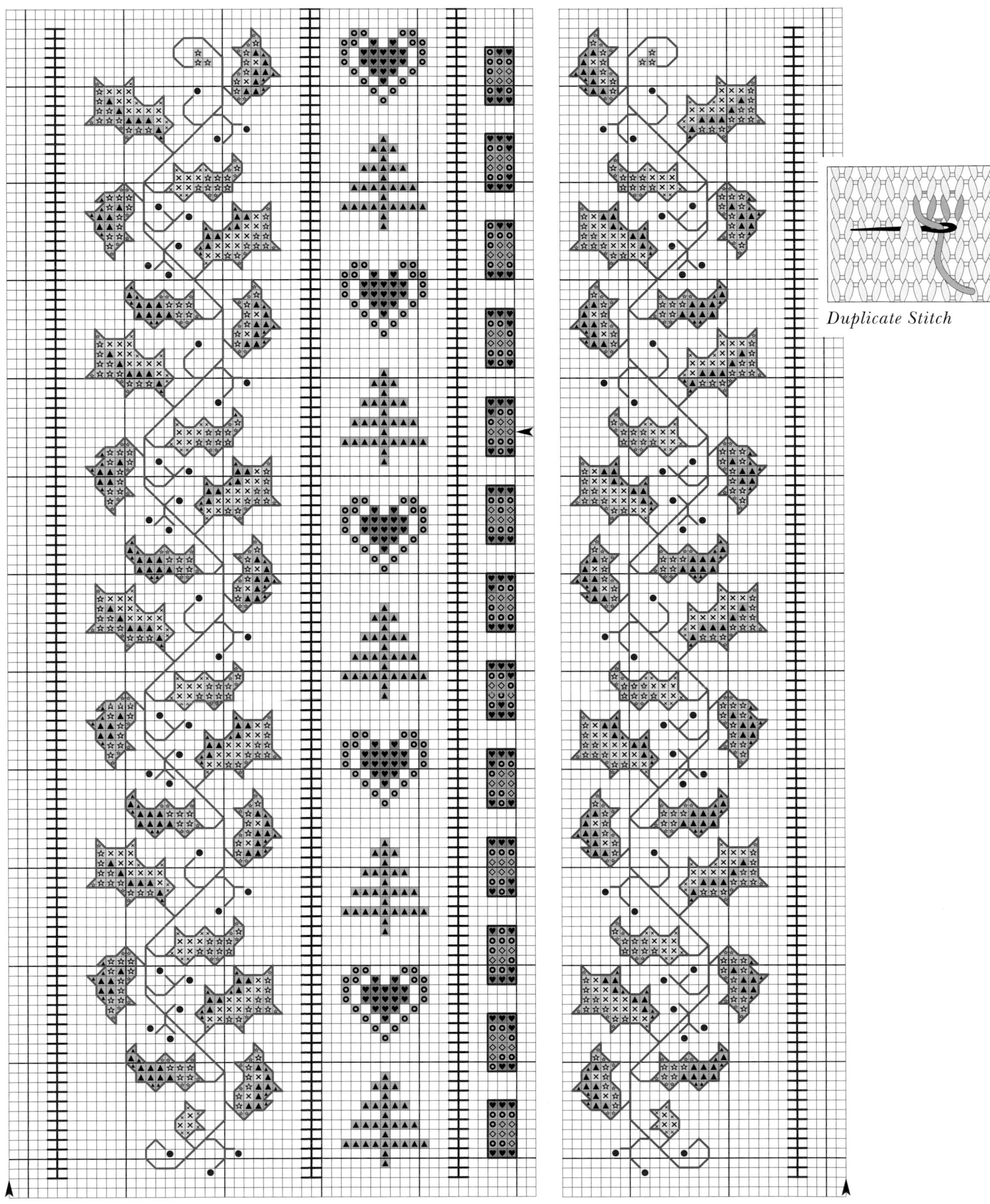


Right Front

Left Front

## Holly Vest

*The chart and key are on pages 40–41.*

### Supplies

*Two—18×30" pieces of 10-count sage green Tula fabric*
*Lined vest pattern with no seams or darts in the front*
*Erasable fabric marker*
*Cotton embroidery floss*
*Caron Collection Watercolours thread*
*Fabric for the vest back and lining*
*Matching sewing thread*
*Three heart-shaped clasps (optional)*

### Stitches

Lay the vest front pattern on one piece of fabric. Trace the outline. Turn the pattern over and trace it onto the remaining fabric. Measure 1⅜" from the bottom center front edge of the right front and begin stitching the left-most row of railroad stitches there.

For railroad stitch, work two vertical backstitches, each over one square of fabric. Then work one straight stitch, perpendicular to the backstitches, over two squares of fabric.

Use three plies of floss for the cross-stitches. Repeat the heart/tree and the rectangle motifs to the shoulder. For the left front piece, work the left front chart in the same manner as the right. Work the heart/tree to the left of it and the rectangle motif to the left of the hearts and trees.

### Assembly

Press pieces from the back. Use the pattern to cut out the pieces. Machine-staystitch or zigzag on the seam lines to prevent raveling. Cut out remaining vest pieces and construct as directed. Sew the clasps to the vest fronts.

## Holiday Heart Mittens

*The chart and key are on pages 40–41.*

### Supplies

*Purchased ivory mittens with a gauge of 9 stitches and 11 rows = 1"*
*Red and grass green RibbonFloss*

### Stitches

Center and duplicate-stitch the first heart from the Holly Vest chart two knitted stitches above the cuff of the mitten using one strand of red RibbonFloss for all stitches. Stitch the trees using one strand of grass green RibbonFloss for all stitches.

## Christmas Sheep Treat Bag

### Supplies

*7" square of 14-count ivory Aida cloth*
*Gentle Art overdyed floss or cotton embroidery floss*
*Mill Hill seed beads*
*1½"-wide sheep button*
*7×15" piece of gold-print fabric*
*13" length of ⅛"-diameter purchased gold twisted cord*
*Crafts glue*

### Stitches

Center and stitch the chart on the Aida cloth. Use three plies of floss to work the stitches unless otherwise specified. If using overdyed floss, work each individual stitch completely before proceeding to the next stitch. Work basting stitches two squares beyond the stitching on all four sides of the design. Press from the back.

### Assembly

Cut out the stitched piece ¼" beyond the basting. Use the stitched piece as a pattern to cut a back and two lining pieces from the gold-print fabric.

Sew the ornament front and back together along the sides and bottom using ¼" seams and leaving the top edge unstitched; turn right side out. Sew the lining pieces together in the same manner, leaving an opening in one side for turning; *do not* turn.

Slip the ornament inside the lining with the seams matching and raw edges even. Sew around the top edges; turn right side out through the opening in the lining. Slip-stitch the opening closed. Tuck the lining into the ornament. Press the ornament.

For the hanger, dab glue on the ends of the cording to prevent fraying. With the ends of the cording even with the bottom of the ornament, hand-stitch the cording over the seams.

## Christmas Sheep Needle Roll

### Supplies

*6×10" piece of 28-count antique ivory linen*
*Gentle Art overdyed floss or cotton embroidery floss*
*Mill Hill seed beads*
*1½"-wide sheep button*
*Polyester fiberfill*
*2—18" lengths of ⅛"-wide burgundy satin ribbon*

### Stitches

Center and stitch the chart on the linen fabric. Use two plies of floss to work the stitches over two threads unless otherwise specified in the key. If using overdyed floss, work each individual stitch completely before proceeding to the next stitch.

For the ribbon casing, count up 30 horizontal threads from the top row of the stitching, then withdraw three horizontal threads.

For the hemstitch over two, count up another 24 horizontal threads from the ribbon row and withdraw three threads. Fold under the top and bottom edge of the fabric two times, so the folded edge of the hem meets the edge of the openwork area; finger press. Refer to the diagram on *page 43* to work the hemstitches along the

### *Christmas Sheep*

| Anchor | Symbol | DMC | Gentle Art Thread | |
|---|---|---|---|---|
| 100 | # | 327 | 0850 | Hyacinth |
| 683 | ♦ | 500 | 0140 | Blue spruce |
| 891 | ○ | 676 | 0420 | Gold leaf |
| 045 | ♥ | 814 | 0310 | Claret |
| 360 | ◘ | 839 | 1110 | Sable |
| BACKSTITCH (1X) | | | | |
| 683 | / | 500 | 0140 | Blue spruce |
| 891 | / | 676 | 0420 | Gold leaf |
| 045 | / | 814 | 0310 | Garnet |
| HEMSTITCH (over 2 threads) | | | | |
| 045 | 777 | 814 | 0310 | Claret (2X) |
| MILL HILL SEED BEADS | | | | |
| 387 | ● | 00123 | | Cream seed bead with Ecru (2X) |
| BUTTON | | | | |
| 100 | X | 327 | 0850 | 1½"-wide Sheep button with Hyacinth (2X) |

***Needleroll stitch count:*** *106 high x 73 wide*
***Needleroll finished design sizes:***
*28-count fabric – 7½ x 5¼ inches*
*32-count fabric – 6⅝ x 4½ inches*
*36-count fabric – 5⅞ x 4 inches*
***Sheep stitch count:*** *44 high x 43 wide*
***Sheep finished design sizes:***
*28-count fabric – 3⅛ x 3 inches*
*32-count fabric – 2¾ x 2⅝ inches*
*36-count fabric – 2½ x 2⅜ inches*

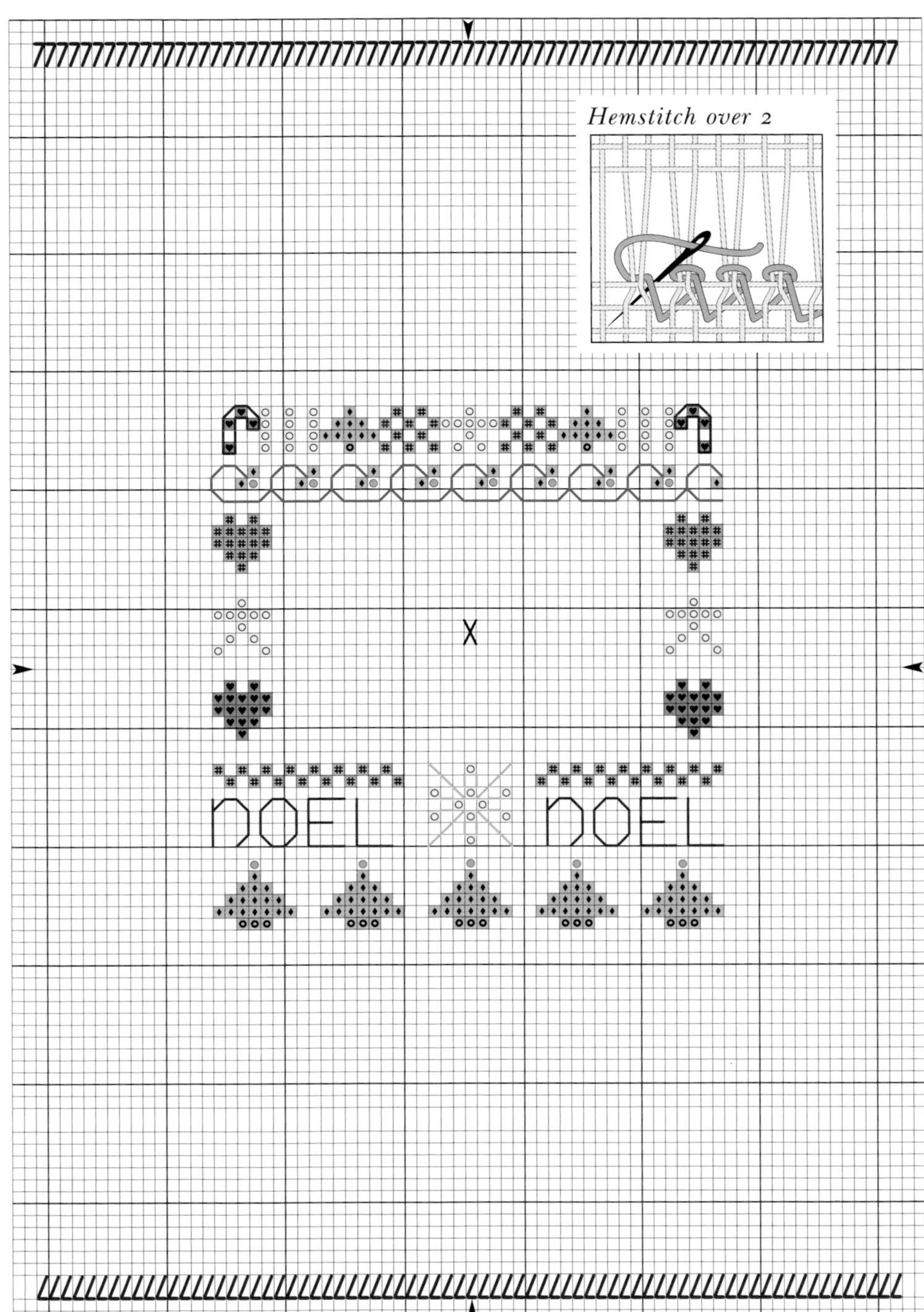


edge of the openwork area, gathering two threads and catching the fold of the hemmed fabric with each stitch. Repeat for the opposite end of the fabric. Attach the seed beads and button as specified in the key. Press from the back.

**Assembly**

With right sides together and raw edges even, sew the long edges of the fabric together with a ¼" seam to make a tube. Turn the fabric right side out. Beginning at the front center of the casing, thread a length of burgundy ribbon through each of the ribbon casings, weaving the ribbon alternately over and under every two threads of the fabric. Stuff the tube firmly with the fiberfill. Tighten the ribbons at each end of the tube and tie them into bows. Trim the ends.

## All Hearts Come Home For Christmas Album

*The chart and key are on pages 44–45.*

**Supplies**

*18×22" piece of 28-count blue ridge linen*
*Cotton embroidery floss*
*Kreinik blending filament*
*Mill Hill seed beads*
*½ yard of 45"-wide salmon cotton fabric*
*½ yard of fleece*
*Matching sewing thread*
*2 yards of ⅛"-diameter metallic gold sew-in piping*
*Graph paper*
*Purchased 11½×10¾×1½" notebook or photo album*

**Stitches**

Chart the desired name onto graph paper using the alphabet and separating the letters with one square. Center and stitch the chart using two plies of floss over two threads of fabric unless otherwise specified in the key. Attach the seed beads using two plies of floss. Press from the back.

**Assembly**

Trim the stitchery ½" beyond the border of the design; set it aside.

Cut a 12¾×24" lining piece from the salmon fabric. Also cut two 2¼×9½" top and bottom sashing strips, a 2×12¾" right side-sashing strip, a 12¾×14½" left side/back piece, and two 6×12¾" inside pockets. Cut a 12¾×24" interlining from the fleece. All measurements include a ½"-seam allowance.

With the right sides together, stitch the top and bottom sashing strips to the stitchery. Sew the right side-sashing strip to the right side of the stitchery. Sew the left side/back to the left side of the stitchery. Center and baste the fleece to the back of the joined pieces. Baste the cording around the album cover, overlapping the ends.

Press one long edge of the inside pocket pieces under ¼" twice; topstitch. Pin an inside pocket to one end of the cover with right sides together; stitch. Repeat for the other side of the cover.

With the right sides together, sew the lining and the front together along the edges, leaving an opening to turn. Trim the seams and clip the corners; turn right side out and press. Slip-stitch the opening closed. Insert the ends of the notebook into the pockets.

All Hearts come Home
for CHRISTMAS

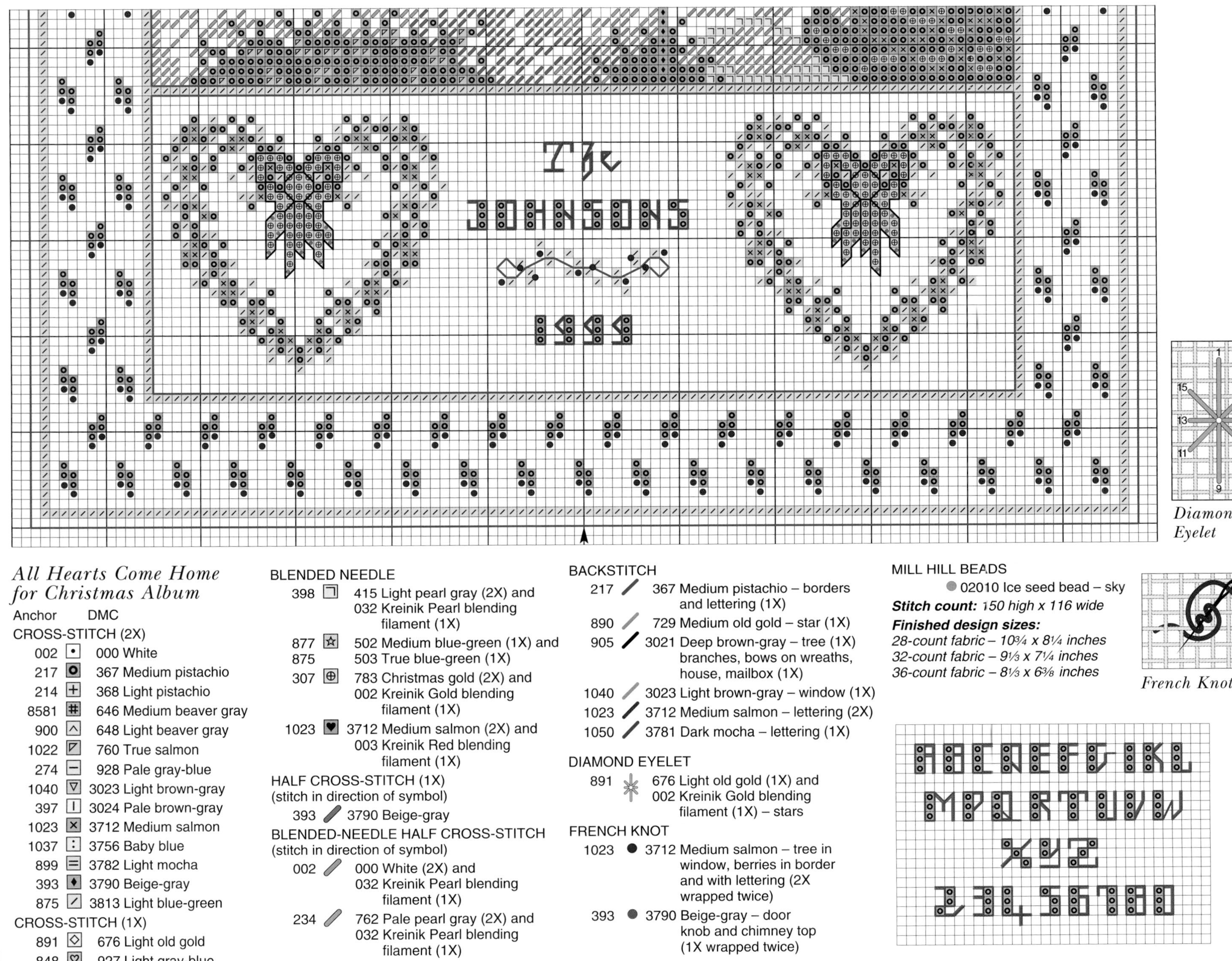


## *All Hearts Come Home for Christmas Album*

Anchor DMC

CROSS-STITCH (2X)

| Anchor | Symbol | DMC |
|---|---|---|
| 002 | • | 000 White |
| 217 | ◘ | 367 Medium pistachio |
| 214 | + | 368 Light pistachio |
| 8581 | # | 646 Medium beaver gray |
| 900 | ^ | 648 Light beaver gray |
| 1022 | ◸ | 760 True salmon |
| 274 | − | 928 Pale gray-blue |
| 1040 | ▽ | 3023 Light brown-gray |
| 397 | I | 3024 Pale brown-gray |
| 1023 | × | 3712 Medium salmon |
| 1037 | : | 3756 Baby blue |
| 899 | ≡ | 3782 Light mocha |
| 393 | ♦ | 3790 Beige-gray |
| 875 | / | 3813 Light blue-green |

CROSS-STITCH (1X)

| Anchor | Symbol | DMC |
|---|---|---|
| 891 | ◇ | 676 Light old gold |
| 848 | ♡ | 927 Light gray-blue |

BLENDED NEEDLE

| Anchor | Symbol | DMC |
|---|---|---|
| 398 | ⌐ | 415 Light pearl gray (2X) and 032 Kreinik Pearl blending filament (1X) |
| 877 / 875 | ☆ | 502 Medium blue-green (1X) and 503 True blue-green (1X) |
| 307 | ⊕ | 783 Christmas gold (2X) and 002 Kreinik Gold blending filament (1X) |
| 1023 | ♥ | 3712 Medium salmon (2X) and 003 Kreinik Red blending filament (1X) |

HALF CROSS-STITCH (1X) (stitch in direction of symbol)

| Anchor | DMC |
|---|---|
| 393 | 3790 Beige-gray |

BLENDED-NEEDLE HALF CROSS-STITCH (stitch in direction of symbol)

| Anchor | DMC |
|---|---|
| 002 | 000 White (2X) and 032 Kreinik Pearl blending filament (1X) |
| 234 | 762 Pale pearl gray (2X) and 032 Kreinik Pearl blending filament (1X) |

BACKSTITCH

| Anchor | DMC |
|---|---|
| 217 | 367 Medium pistachio – borders and lettering (1X) |
| 890 | 729 Medium old gold – star (1X) |
| 905 | 3021 Deep brown-gray – tree (1X) branches, bows on wreaths, house, mailbox (1X) |
| 1040 | 3023 Light brown-gray – window (1X) |
| 1023 | 3712 Medium salmon – lettering (2X) |
| 1050 | 3781 Dark mocha – lettering (1X) |

DIAMOND EYELET

| Anchor | DMC |
|---|---|
| 891 | 676 Light old gold (1X) and 002 Kreinik Gold blending filament (1X) – stars |

FRENCH KNOT

| Anchor | DMC |
|---|---|
| 1023 | 3712 Medium salmon – tree in window, berries in border and with lettering (2X wrapped twice) |
| 393 | 3790 Beige-gray – door knob and chimney top (1X wrapped twice) |

MILL HILL BEADS

● 02010 Ice seed bead – sky

**Stitch count:** *150 high x 116 wide*

**Finished design sizes:**
*28-count fabric – 10¾ x 8¼ inches*
*32-count fabric – 9⅓ x 7¼ inches*
*36-count fabric – 8⅓ x 6⅜ inches*

# Stockings &

# Stuffers

*The Christmas Eve tradition of filling stockings with gifts and treats has been cherished for generations. This year, include lovingly stitched socks and fanciful gifts as you share this enchanting Christmas custom.*

Here's a stocking that says "Christmas." Each row of holiday images is suitable for holiday gift and decorating projects. Choose from several stocking styles. Work the cuff on a contrasting color as shown *opposite,* or stitch the entire stocking on the same fabric. Stitch only the cuff on banding to top a sparkly lamé or plush velvet stocking.

For decorating, center the bells or any of the stocking bands on crochet-edge Aida-cloth banding to make a lacy shelf edging, *above.* Stitch a quick holiday memento using a single motif tucked into a flanged pillow, *right.* Look for more ideas on *pages 58–59.*

*Design: Barbara Sestok*

Celebrate the holidays with Scottish style. Highland Santa, a charming Christmas character, has gift ideas galore. Stitch the stocking, *opposite,* on rustic Linaida cloth and embellish it with jingle bells. Stitch the Santa figure alone on a woven plaid square and finish as a pillow, *above*. Or, borrow one of the plaid borders to edge a bread cover, *right*. Look for more gift ideas on *pages 62–63*.

*Design: Robin Clark*

THOMAS
by R.B.C. 1999

JEFFREY
let it Snow!

It's snowing stockings, and you can pick your favorite. Stitch the 16" stocking with five charming snow people, *opposite,* on 14-count white Aida cloth. Choose a pewter evenweave fabric for the 9½" stockings, *above.* They have the same heart- and star-studded cuff, a checked toe, and your choice of motifs from the larger design.

*Design: Robin Kingsley*

Make this Christmas personal. Tuck a customized pocket pal into every stocking on your mantel. The key includes color options so you can adjust the skin, eye, and hair color of the children, as well as the fur color of the bears. Fill each with plastic pellets for a bean-bag feel.

*Design: Robin Clark*

## Holiday Borders Stocking

*The chart and key are on pages 56–57.*

### Supplies

*18×24" piece of 28-count amaretto Jubilee fabric*
*10×18" piece of 28-count blueberry Annabelle fabric*
*Cotton embroidery floss*
*Mill Hill seed beads*
*Erasable fabric marker*
*½ yard of 45"-wide tan cotton fabric*
*¼ yard of 45"-wide blue cotton fabric*
*1½ yards of ⅛"-diameter cording or purchased piping*

### Stitches

Center and stitch the stocking body on the Jubilee fabric using three plies of floss over two threads of fabric unless otherwise specified.

Center and stitch the stocking cuff on the Annabelle fabric using three plies of floss over two threads of fabric unless otherwise specified. Press the stitched pieces from the back.

### Assembly

Use the marker to draw the stocking outline as indicated by the dashed black line on the chart. Cut out the stocking ½" beyond the drawn line. Use the stocking as a pattern to cut one back and two lining pieces from the tan fabric and to cut one matching piece from fleece.

Use the marker to draw the cuff outlines indicated by the red dashed lines, extending each line 3" to the left and right of the stitching. Draw a vertical line connecting the ends of the first two lines on each side. (The stitched design will be centered horizontally on a 4¼×13½" rectangle.) Cut out the cuff ½" beyond the outline. Use it as a pattern to cut a lining from the blue cotton fabric. From the blue Annabelle or cotton fabric, cut enough 1¼"-wide strips to make 45" of piping.

Baste the fleece to the back of the stitched stocking. Sew short ends of the piping strips together. Center the cording lengthwise on the wrong side of the piping. Fold the fabric around the cording with raw edges even. Use a zipper foot to sew through the layers close to the cording.

Baste the piping to the stocking front. With right sides together, stitch the stocking front and back together, clip curves, and turn right side out.

Sew the lining pieces together with right sides together, leaving an opening near the toe; *do not* turn.

For the cuff, with right sides together, stitch the cuff and lining together along the bottom edge only, following the stitching to create the scallops. Clip curves and trim the seam to ¼" and press toward the lining. Open the lining and cuff to form one layer of fabric. With right sides together stitch the center back seam, press the seam open, and turn right side out.

Baste the cuff to the top of the stocking. Insert the stocking with cuff into the stocking lining. Stitch around the top edge. Turn right side out, sew opening in foot of lining closed and tuck the lining into the stocking.

## Snowman and Gingerbread Pin Cushions

*The chart and key are on pages 56–57.*

### Supplies

***For each pin cushion or ornament***
*6" square of Fiddler's Lite light oatmeal 14-count Aida cloth*
*Purchased Tiny Tuck pillow with a 2" square opening*
*Cotton embroidery floss*
*Metallic embroidery floss (optional)*
*Mill Hill seed beads*

### Stitches

Center and stitch one gingerbread or snowman motif from the Holiday Borders Stocking chart on the Aida cloth using three plies of floss unless otherwise specified.

### Assembly

Centering the design, cut the Aida cloth to measure 3½" square. If desired, cut the fabric on the bias. Carefully tuck the edges of the fabric under the flanges of the pillow.

Using two strands of embroidery floss in a color that harmonizes with the fabric, work blanket stitches around the edge of the cross-stitch fabric. If desired, add beads to every third stitch.

## Bell Shelf Liner

*The chart and key are on pages 56–57.*

### Supplies

*16-count 4"-wide white Aida-cloth banding with red crochet edge to fit desired shelf plus 1"*
*Cotton embroidery floss*

### Stitches

Measure ½" from the end of the banding. Center the bell motif from the Holiday Borders Stocking chart and stitch using two plies of floss and omitting beads.

*As a pin cushion or an ornament, either of these quick-to-stitch characters from the Holiday Borders Stocking becomes a memorable gift.*

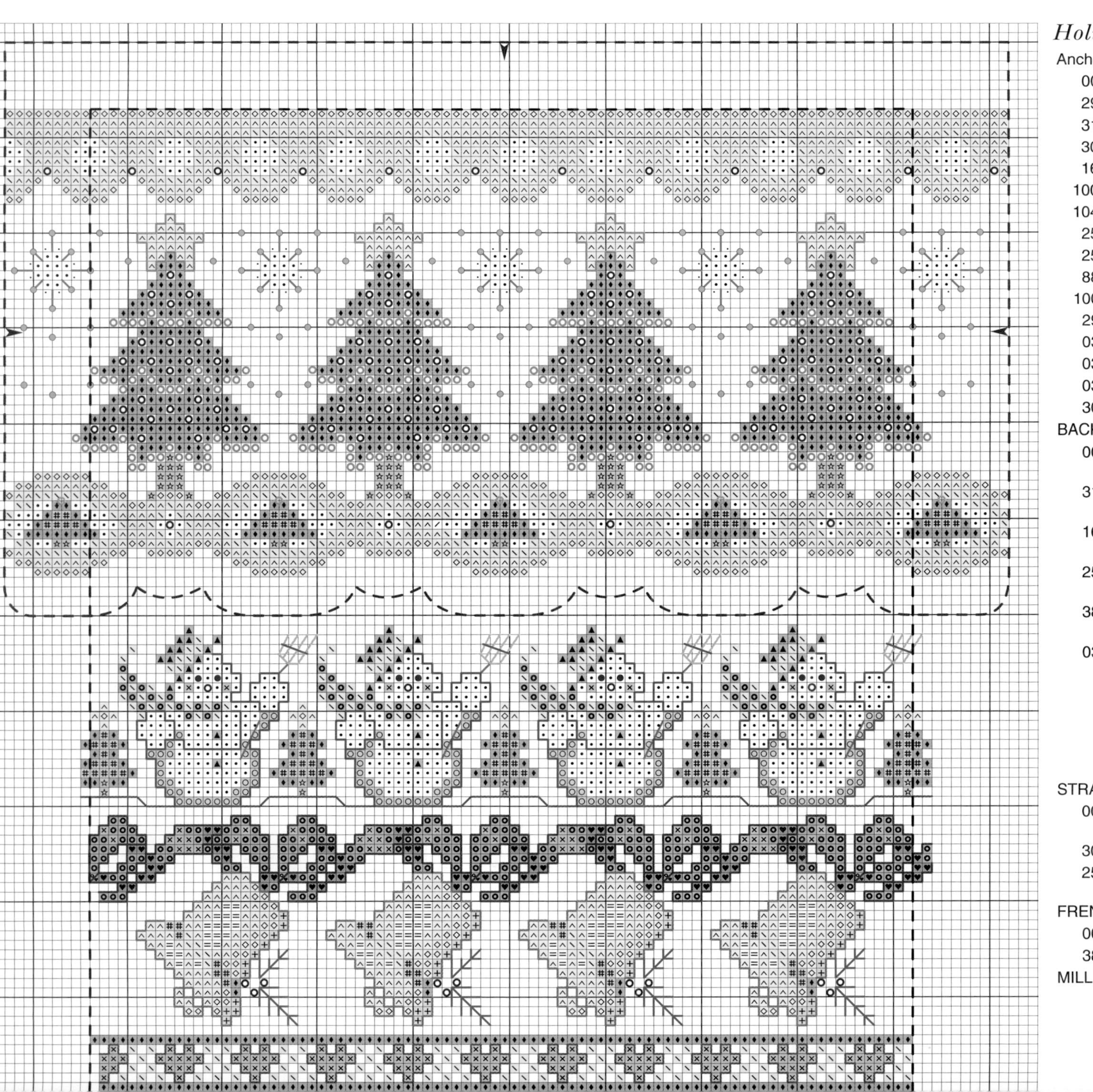

## *Holiday Borders Stocking*

| Anchor | | DMC |
|---|---|---|
| 002 | • | 000 White |
| 295 | ^ | 726 Light topaz |
| 310 | ▲ | 780 Deep topaz |
| 307 | + | 783 Christmas gold |
| 161 | ○ | 813 Powder blue |
| 1005 | ♥ | 816 Garnet |
| 1044 | ♦ | 895 Hunter green |
| 257 | # | 905 Dark parrot green |
| 255 | \ | 907 Light parrot green |
| 881 | – | 945 Ivory |
| 1001 | ☆ | 976 Golden brown |
| 292 | = | 3078 Lemon |
| 033 | × | 3706 Medium watermelon |
| 031 | ♡ | 3708 Light watermelon |
| 035 | ◉ | 3801 Deep watermelon |
| 306 | ◇ | 3820 Straw |

BACKSTITCH (1X)

- 002 / 000 White – gingerbread men, houses, and heart
- 310 / 780 Deep topaz – bells, snowman broom handle
- 161 / 813 Powder blue – snowmen, trim on Santa's hat and coat
- 257 / 905 Dark parrot green – Santa's bag and boots
- 381 / 938 Coffee brown – jingle bells, Santa detail, ribbons
- 031 / 3708 Light watermelon – gingerbread house roof and gingerbread men
- / 5282 Metallic gold – stars, holly leaves, patchwork motifs
- / 5283 Metallic silver – line under snowmen, small hearts, greens near patchwork motifs

STRAIGHT STITCH (1X)

- 002 / 000 White – Santa's eyebrows, snowflakes
- 307 / 783 Christmas gold – broom
- 257 / 905 Dark parrot green – greens on bells and broom

FRENCH KNOT (1X wrapped once)

- 002 ● 000 White – snowflakes
- 381 ● 938 Coffee brown – eyes

MILL HILL BEADS

- ○ 00167 Christmas green seed beads – large trees and border above gingerbread men

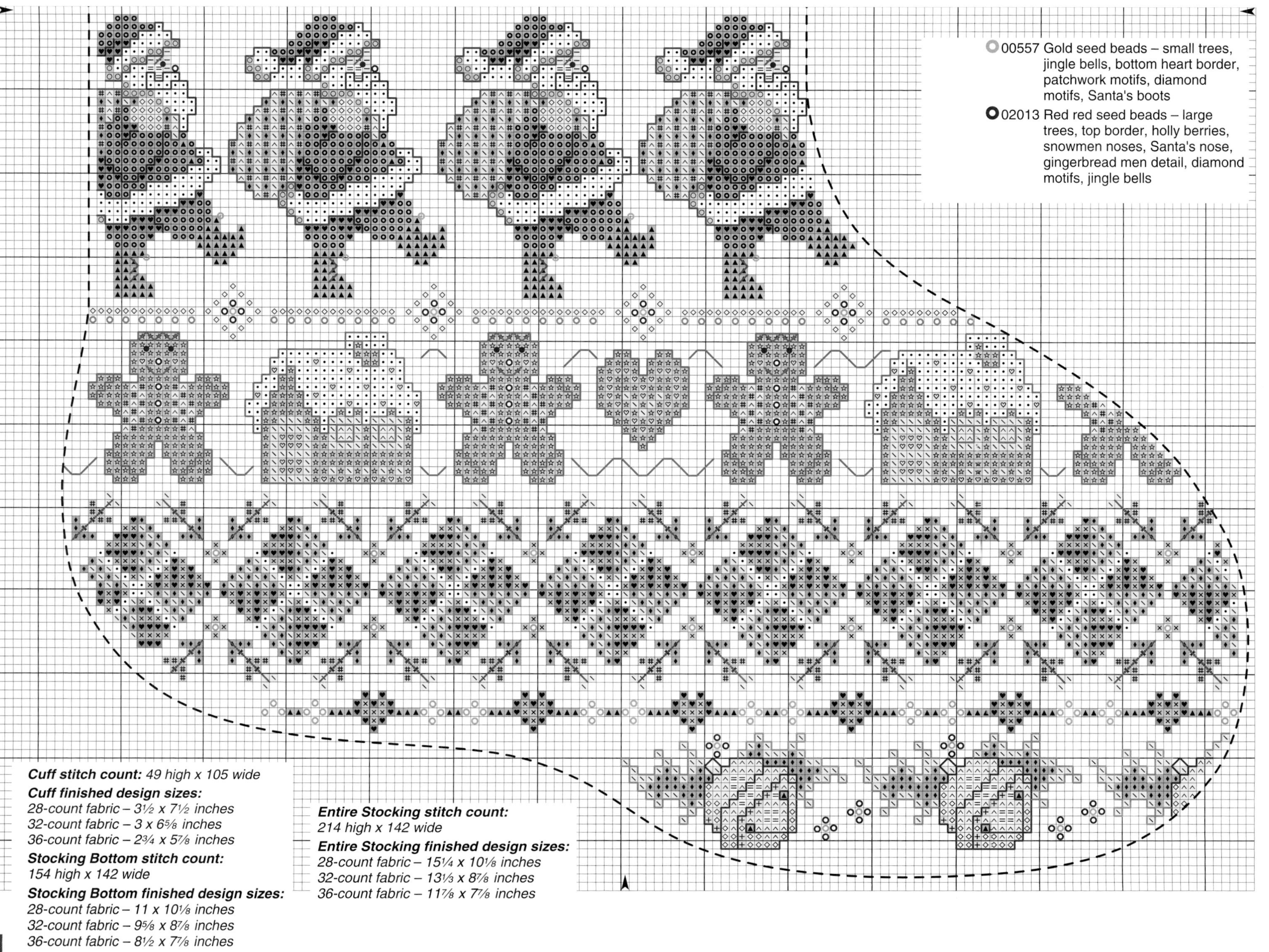


**Cuff stitch count:** *49 high x 105 wide*

**Cuff finished design sizes:**
*28-count fabric – 3½ x 7½ inches*
*32-count fabric – 3 x 6⅝ inches*
*36-count fabric – 2¾ x 5⅞ inches*

**Stocking Bottom stitch count:**
*154 high x 142 wide*

**Stocking Bottom finished design sizes:**
*28-count fabric – 11 x 10⅛ inches*
*32-count fabric – 9⅝ x 8⅞ inches*
*36-count fabric – 8½ x 7⅞ inches*

**Entire Stocking stitch count:**
*214 high x 142 wide*

**Entire Stocking finished design sizes:**
*28-count fabric – 15¼ x 10⅛ inches*
*32-count fabric – 13⅓ x 8⅞ inches*
*36-count fabric – 11⅞ x 7⅞ inches*

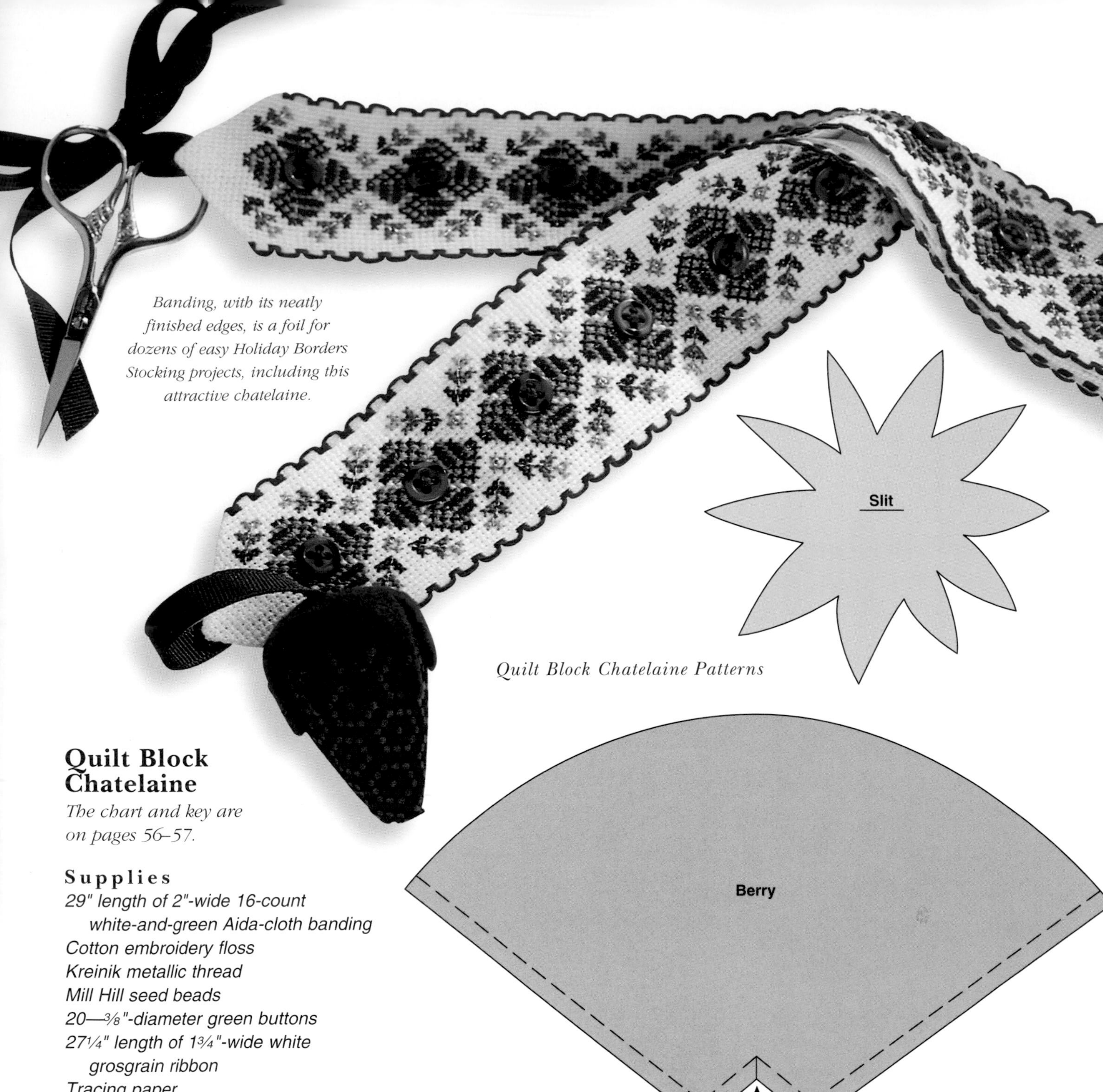


*Banding, with its neatly finished edges, is a foil for dozens of easy Holiday Borders Stocking projects, including this attractive chatelaine.*

*Quilt Block Chatelaine Patterns*

## Quilt Block Chatelaine

*The chart and key are on pages 56–57.*

### Supplies

*29" length of 2"-wide 16-count white-and-green Aida-cloth banding*
*Cotton embroidery floss*
*Kreinik metallic thread*
*Mill Hill seed beads*
*20—3/8"-diameter green buttons*
*27¼" length of 1¾"-wide white grosgrain ribbon*
*Tracing paper*
*5" square of red-print cotton fabric*
*3" square of dark green felt*
*Polyester fiberfill*
*26" length of 3/8"-wide dark green grosgrain ribbon*

### Stitches

Measure 1¾" from one end of the banding. Center and stitch the quilt-block motif from the Holiday Borders Stocking chart using two plies of floss unless otherwise specified. Repeat the block twenty times, ending 1¾" from the end of the banding.

### Assembly

Use matching floss to sew a button to the center of each quilt block.

Trim the ends of banding 1" beyond the stitched area. To shape the points, fold one end of the banding in half lengthwise, right sides together. Measure 1" from the raw edge of the banding and make a mark. Sew diagonally across the banding from the fold to the mark. Trim the seam, press open and turn. Fold into a point by matching the seam to the vertical center of the banding. Repeat at the other end of the banding and both ends of the 1¾"-wide grosgrain ribbon. Set the pieces aside.

Trace the berry and leaf cap patterns, *above,* onto tracing paper; cut out. Cut one berry from the red-print fabric and one leaf cap from the dark green felt.

Fold the berry in half with right sides together. Sew along the tip and straight edge of the berry, leaving the curved edge open. Clip the fabric at the tip of the berry; turn right side out. Work a row of gathering stitches ⅛" from the curved edge of berry. Stuff the berry firmly, using tiny pieces of

fiberfill. Tighten the gathering threads, adding fiberfill to round out the top of the berry. Pull the threads tightly until there is almost no opening at the top of the berry; knot securely.

Cut a 4" length of ⅜"-wide dark green ribbon. Sew one end of ribbon to the top of the berry. Cut the slit in the leaf cap and thread the ribbon through it. Tack the leaf points to the berry with French knots, using six plies of dark pistachio floss (DMC 319) wrapped once around the needle. Sew the other end of the green ribbon to the wrong side of one end of the white ribbon.

Fold the remaining green grosgrain ribbon in half. Sew the folded end of the ribbon to the wrong side of the remaining white ribbon.

With wrong sides together, center and hand- or machine-stitch the banding over the white ribbon.

## Tree and Snowflake Paperweight

*The chart and key are on pages 56–57.*

### Supplies

*9½×8" piece of 25-count raw linen Dublin linen*
*Cotton embroidery floss*
*Kreinik blending filament*
*2¾×4⅛" purchased glass paperweight*

### Stitches

Center and stitch the Holiday Borders cuff chart omitting the tree on the right and the portion of each border immediately above and below it. Use one ply of floss to work cross-stitches and backstitches over one thread. Omit the beads. Press from the back.

### Assembly

Assemble according to instructions included with the paperweight.

## Highland Santa Stocking

*The chart and key are on pages 60–61.*

### Supplies

*27×18" piece of 14-count Linaida cloth*
*Cotton embroidery floss*
*Graph paper*
*Erasable fabric marker*
*1 yard of 45"-wide burgundy moiré taffeta fabric*
*½ yard of fusible fleece*
*1¼ yards of ⅛"-diameter cording*
*Matching sewing threads*
*Metallic gold sewing thread*
*33—¼"-diameter gold jingle bells*

### Stitches

Use the alphabet on *page 62* to chart the desired name, separating each letter with one square. Center and stitch the chart on the fabric using three plies of floss unless otherwise specified. Press from the back.

### Assembly

Fuse the fleece to the back of the stitched piece following the manufacturer's instructions. Use the marker to draw the stocking outline as indicated by the green line. Cut out the stocking ½" beyond the outline.

Use the stocking as a pattern to cut one back and two lining pieces from the burgundy fabric. Also cut a ¾×6½" hanging strip, a 7×15¾" cuff, and enough ¾"-wide strips to make 1¼ yards of piping from the burgundy fabric. Cut a 3½×15¾" cuff interlining from the fleece.

For the piping, sew the strips together. Center the cording lengthwise on the wrong side of the piping strip. Fold the fabric around the cording with the raw edges together. Using

*Show off tiny stitches through the lens of a ready-to-finish paperweight.*

a zipper foot, sew close to the cording through both fabric layers. Baste the piping around the sides and foot of the stocking with the raw edges even.

Sew the stocking front to the back along the basting lines, leaving the top edge open. Turn right side out and press. Sew the lining pieces together, right sides facing, leaving the top open; *do not* turn. Slip the lining inside the stocking. With raw edges even, baste the stocking to the lining at the top edges; press carefully. Set the stocking aside.

Press the cuff in half lengthwise, wrong sides together. Open the fabric, and fuse the fleece to one side of the cuff. On the fleece-lined portion (front) of the cuff, measure and mark a diagonal grid at 1" intervals. Machine-quilt along the marked lines using metallic gold sewing thread.

Sew the short ends of the cuff together, right sides facing; press the seam open. Hand-sew a jingle bell at each intersection of the grid on the front of the cuff.

With right sides together, sew the raw edge of the cuff front to the top of the stocking. Press the seam toward the cuff. Press the raw edge of the cuff back under ½". Fold the cuff back to the inside of the stocking and slipstitch the edge to the cuff seam.

*Continued*

## Highland Santa Stocking

| Anchor | Symbol | DMC |
|---|---|---|
| 002 | • | 000 White |
| 897 | # | 221 Shell pink |
| 403 | ■ | 310 Black |
| 1019 | ♦ | 315 Dark antique mauve |
| 1025 | ◎ | 347 Deep salmon |
| 1014 | ⊕ | 355 Dark terra-cotta |
| 683 | ● | 500 Blue-green |
| 860 | I | 522 Olive drab |
| 8581 | × | 646 Medium beaver gray |
| 900 | ♡ | 648 Light beaver gray |
| 361 | + | 738 Light tan |
| 885 | ^ | 739 Pale tan |
| 301 | – | 744 Yellow |
| 1022 | ○ | 760 True salmon |
| 045 | ♥ | 814 Garnet |
| 945 | ✱ | 834 Bronze |
| 218 | ▲ | 890 Pistachio |
| 862 | ★ | 934 Pine green |
| 681 | ⁘ | 3051 Gray-green |
| 292 | ▽ | 3078 Lemon |
| 1024 | ◗ | 3328 Dark salmon |
| 1023 | □ | 3712 Medium salmon |
| 1018 | = | 3726 True antique mauve |
| 872 | ◇ | 3740 Antique violet |
| 1036 | ⦶ | 3750 Antique blue |
| 868 | ∾ | 3779 Pale terra-cotta |
| 1050 | ⋈ | 3781 Mocha |

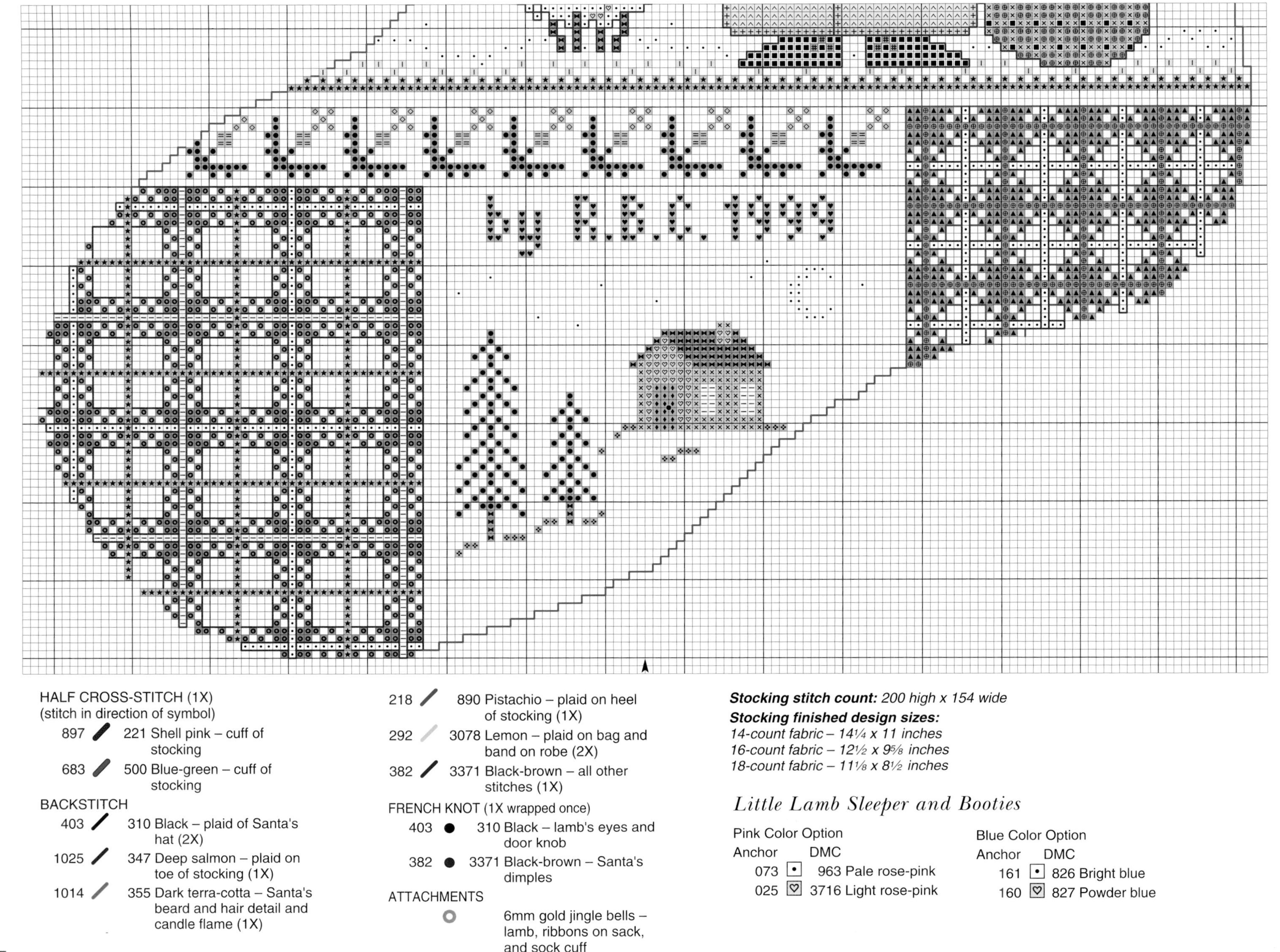


HALF CROSS-STITCH (1X)
(stitch in direction of symbol)

| Anchor | DMC |
|---|---|
| 897 | 221 Shell pink – cuff of stocking |
| 683 | 500 Blue-green – cuff of stocking |

BACKSTITCH

| Anchor | DMC |
|---|---|
| 403 | 310 Black – plaid of Santa's hat (2X) |
| 1025 | 347 Deep salmon – plaid on toe of stocking (1X) |
| 1014 | 355 Dark terra-cotta – Santa's beard and hair detail and candle flame (1X) |
| 218 | 890 Pistachio – plaid on heel of stocking (1X) |
| 292 | 3078 Lemon – plaid on bag and band on robe (2X) |
| 382 | 3371 Black-brown – all other stitches (1X) |

FRENCH KNOT (1X wrapped once)

| Anchor | DMC |
|---|---|
| 403 | 310 Black – lamb's eyes and door knob |
| 382 | 3371 Black-brown – Santa's dimples |

ATTACHMENTS

6mm gold jingle bells – lamb, ribbons on sack, and sock cuff

***Stocking stitch count:*** *200 high x 154 wide*
***Stocking finished design sizes:***
*14-count fabric – 14¼ x 11 inches*
*16-count fabric – 12½ x 9⅝ inches*
*18-count fabric – 11⅛ x 8½ inches*

## *Little Lamb Sleeper and Booties*

Pink Color Option

| Anchor | DMC |
|---|---|
| 073 | 963 Pale rose-pink |
| 025 | 3716 Light rose-pink |

Blue Color Option

| Anchor | DMC |
|---|---|
| 161 | 826 Bright blue |
| 160 | 827 Powder blue |

Press the long edges of the hanging strip under ¼". Fold the strip in half lengthwise; topstitch close to the fold. Fold the strip in half to form a loop. Tack the loop inside the top right edge of the cuff.

*For yourself or as a gift, this bread cloth earns important accolades—pretty, practical, and easy to stitch.*

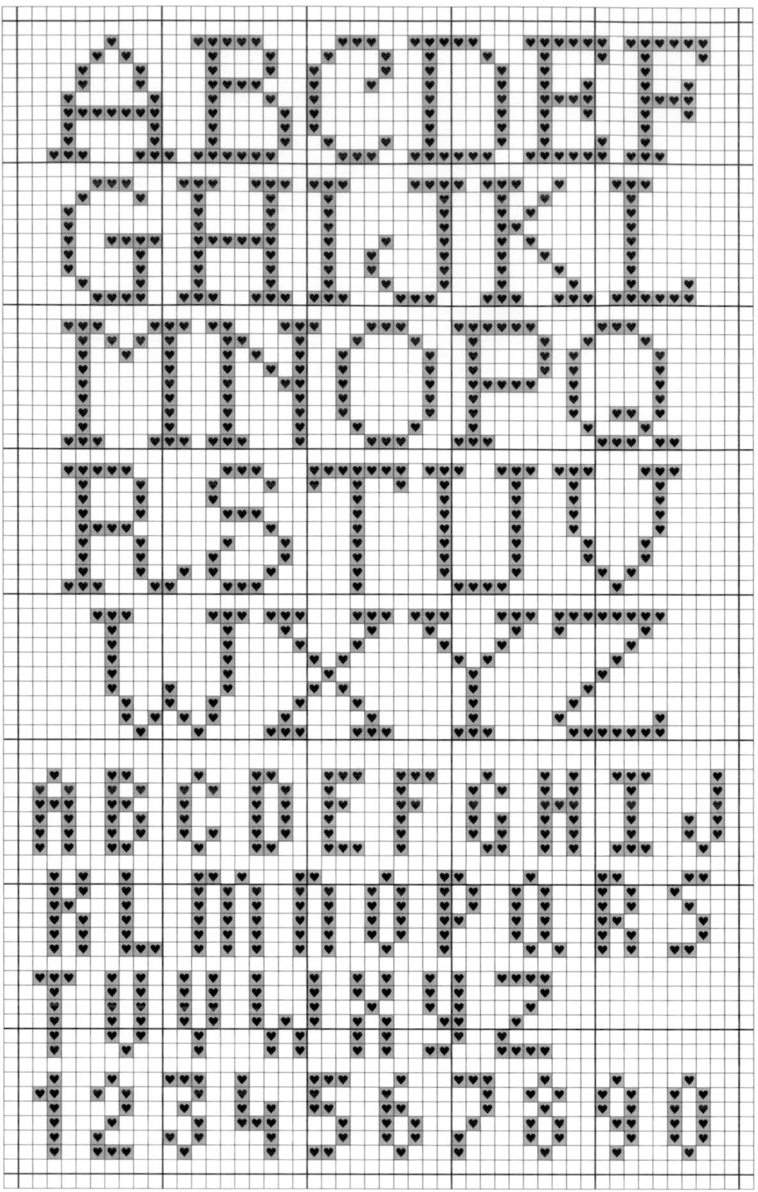

*Highland Santa Stocking Alphabet*

## Tartan Border Bread Cloth

*The chart and key are on pages 60–61.*

### Supplies

*18×18" prefinished country oatmeal bread cover*
*Cotton embroidery floss*

### Stitches

Measure ⅞" from one corner of the bread cover. Begin stitching the plaid border from the Highland Santa Stocking chart there, using three plies of floss and repeating the pattern as necessary to reach the opposite edge. Return to the same corner and stitch the border across the adjoining edge.

## Highland Santa Pillow

*The chart and key are on pages 60–61.*

### Supplies

*15" square of 14-count hunter-and-tea on natural Cornerblock fabric*
*Cotton embroidery floss*
*½ yard of 45"-wide small-check fabric*
*2 yards of ¼"-diameter cording*
*Purchased 14" square pillow form*

### Stitches

Center and stitch the Santa figure from the Highland Santa Stocking chart on the fabric using three plies of floss unless otherwise specified. Press from the back.

### Assembly

If necessary, trim the fabric to a 15" square. From the check fabric, cut one 15" square pillow back. Also cut enough 1½"-wide bias strips of fabric to equal 60" in length. Sew the short ends of bias strips together to make one long piece. Center the cording lengthwise on the wrong side of the piping strip. Fold the fabric around the cording, bringing the raw edges together. Using a zipper foot, sew close to the cording through both layers. Baste the piping to the right side of the stitchery, overlapping the ends at the center bottom.

Sew the pillow front and back together with right sides facing, leaving an opening for turning. Clip the corners; turn right side out. Press the pillow. Insert the pillow form and slip-stitch the opening closed.

## Thistle Earrings

*The chart and key are on pages 60–61.*

### Supplies

*2—6" squares of 18-count white Aida cloth*
*Cotton embroidery floss*
*2—⅞"-diameter button cover forms*
*Wire cutters*
*2—2½" squares of fusible interfacing*
*Crafts glue*
*Earring findings*
*All-purpose adhesive*

*Scottish or not, the lassie on your list will appreciate these thistle earrings.*

### Stitches

Center and stitch one large thistle from the Highland Santa Stocking chart on each piece of fabric. Use two plies of floss unless otherwise specified. Press from the back.

### Assembly

Center and fuse interfacing on the back of each stitched piece following the manufacturer's instructions.

Center the design over the button form. Trim the fabric ½" beyond the edge. Run a gathering thread ¼" from the cut edge. Pull up the gathers to smooth the fabric.

Assemble the button following the manufacturer's instructions. Use wire cutters to remove the metal shank from the back of each button form.

For the twisted cord, cut 1-yard lengths of dark gray-green (DMC 3051) and dark garnet (DMC 814) floss. Combine four plies of gray-green and six plies of garnet into a single strand; knot one end. Twist the strand until it's tightly wound. Holding the ends, fold the strand in half as the two halves twist around each other. Glue the unfinished end to secure. Glue the twisted cord around the edges of the earring, overlapping the ends. Glue the ends to the back. Cement the earring findings to the earring backs.

## Little Lamb Sleeper and Booties

*The chart and key are on pages 60–61.*

### Supplies

*Purchased baby sleeper*
*4½" square of 11- or 12-count waste canvas*
*Purchased 14-count white Royal Classic baby booties*
*Cotton embroidery floss*
*Pink or blue ⅛"-wide satin ribbon*

### Stitches

Position and baste the waste canvas to the sleeper as desired. Center and stitch the lamb from the Highland Santa chart using three plies of floss unless otherwise specified.

Center and stitch the lamb motif on the bottom of each bootie using an alternate key if desired. Center a lamb's head on each bootie toe four squares below the cuff.

### Assembly

Remove the basting and trim the canvas close to the stitching. Wet the canvas slightly. Use tweezers to remove the threads of the waste canvas. Thread the ribbon under the center stitch of the lamb's bow; tie the ends in a small bow. Trim the ends.

*Need a gift for baby's first Christmas? You can stitch Highland Santa's lamb in pink, blue, or white on a cuddly sleeper and matching booties.*

Let It Snow Stocking

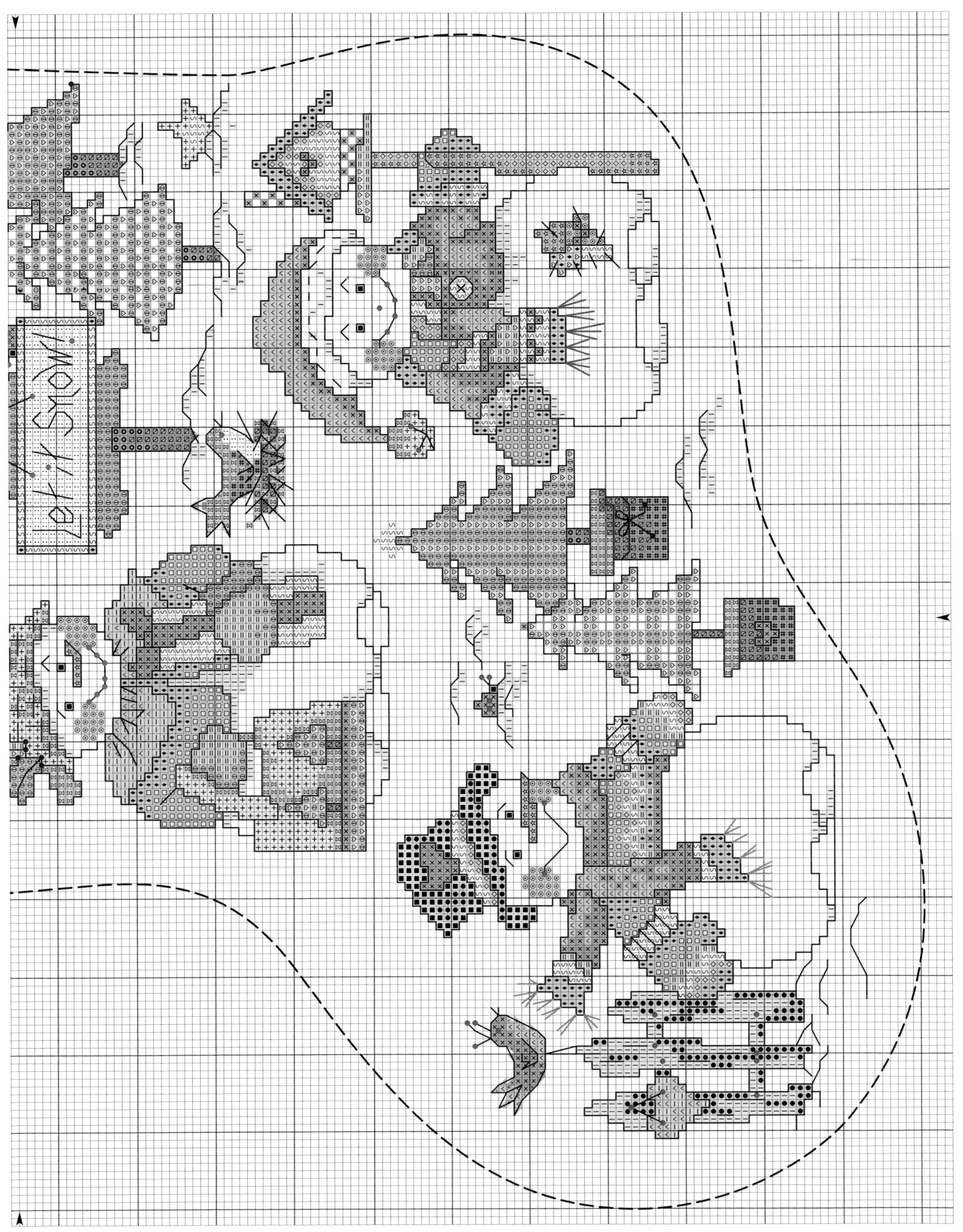

## *Let It Snow Stocking*

| Anchor | | DMC |
|---|---|---|
| 1049 | ◪ | 301 Mahogany |
| 403 | ■ | 310 Black |
| 9046 | ☒ | 321 Christmas red |
| 010 | ⌃ | 351 Coral |
| 008 | ⊟ | 353 Peach |
| 235 | ● | 414 Steel |
| 398 | ⎕ | 415 Pearl gray |
| 891 | ⊞ | 676 Light old gold |
| 228 | ⦶ | 700 Medium Christmas green |
| 226 | ⊜ | 702 Light Christmas green |
| 256 | ♡ | 704 Chartreuse |
| 324 | ☆ | 721 Medium bittersweet |
| 323 | ◇ | 722 Light bittersweet |
| 295 | S | 726 Topaz |
| 890 | ⧗ | 729 Medium old gold |
| 275 | ⁚ | 746 Off-white |
| 1022 | ◎ | 760 Salmon |
| 161 | ◻ | 813 Powder blue |
| 162 | ♦ | 825 Bright blue |
| 355 | ◉ | 975 Deep golden brown |
| 1001 | # | 976 Medium golden brown |

BACKSTITCH

| | | |
|---|---|---|
| 9046 | / | 321 Christmas red – name and bow on Christmas tree pot (1X) |
| 295 | / | 726 Topaz – top of tree near sign (1X) |
| 890 | / | 729 Medium old gold – tree at the bottom (2X) |
| 403 | / | 310 Black – all remaining stitches (1X) |

STRAIGHT STITCH

| | | |
|---|---|---|
| 403 | / | 310 Black – stitches on patches, bird's feet on fence, nests, heart strings on fence, and "let it snow" sign hangers (1X) |

LAZY DAISY

| | | |
|---|---|---|
| 403 | 0 | 310 Black – hangers on hearts and stars (1X) |
| 9046 | 0 | 321 Christmas red – bow on Christmas tree pot (1X) |

FRENCH KNOT (1X wrapped once)

| | | |
|---|---|---|
| 403 | ● | 310 Black – birds' eyes, top of birds' crest, jingle bell, mouths, nose, ladybugs, sign, hanger on heart, and fence |
| 9046 | ● | 321 Christmas red – holly berries, tree by sign, snowlady apron, bow on Christmas tree pot |
| 295 | ● | 726 Topaz – top of tree near sign |

TURKEY-WORK

| | | |
|---|---|---|
| 226 | / | 702 Light Christmas green – ends of scarf (3X) |
| 295 | / | 726 Topaz – ends of scarf (3X) |

***Stitch count:*** *232 high x 150 wide*

***Finished design sizes:***
*14-count fabric – 16½ x 10¾ inches*
*16-count fabric – 14½ x 9⅜ inches*
*18-count fabric – 12⅞ x 8⅓ inches*

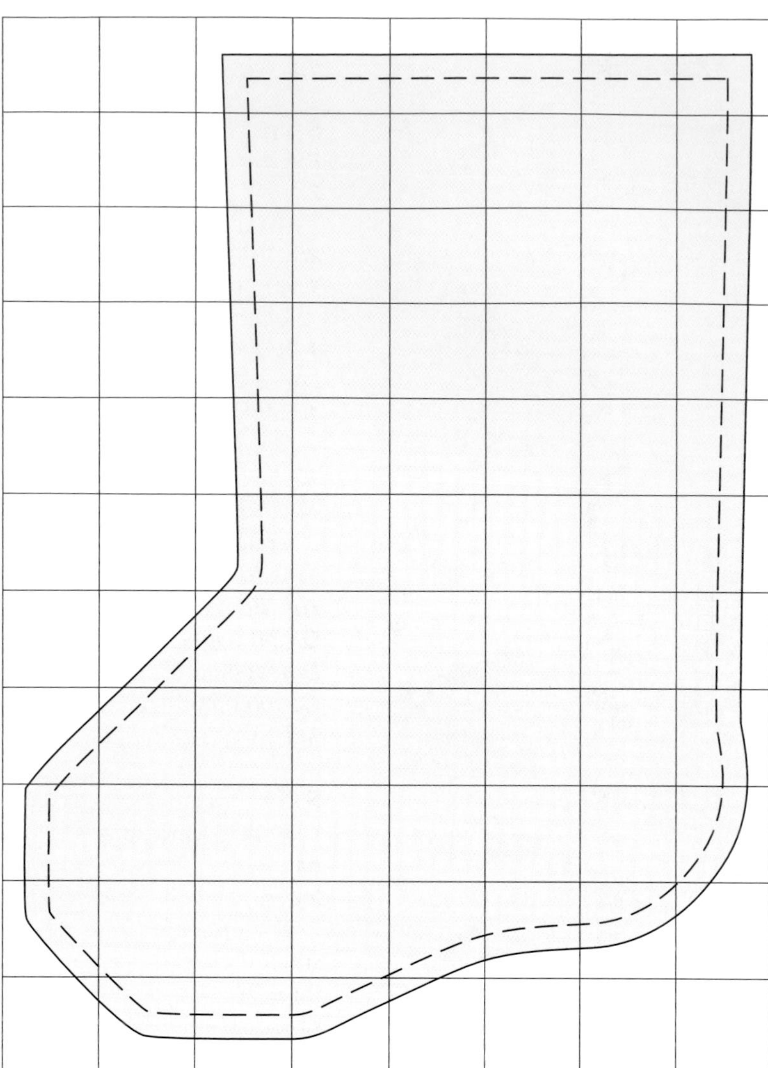

*Let It Snow Small Stocking Pattern* **1 Square = 1 Inch**

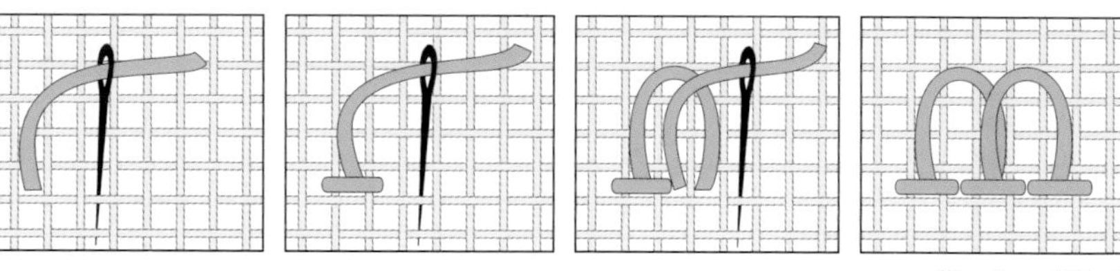

*Turkey-Work*

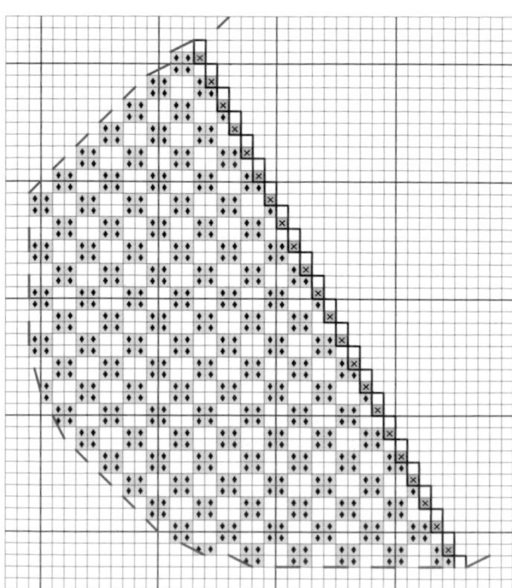

*Let It Snow Small Stocking Toe*

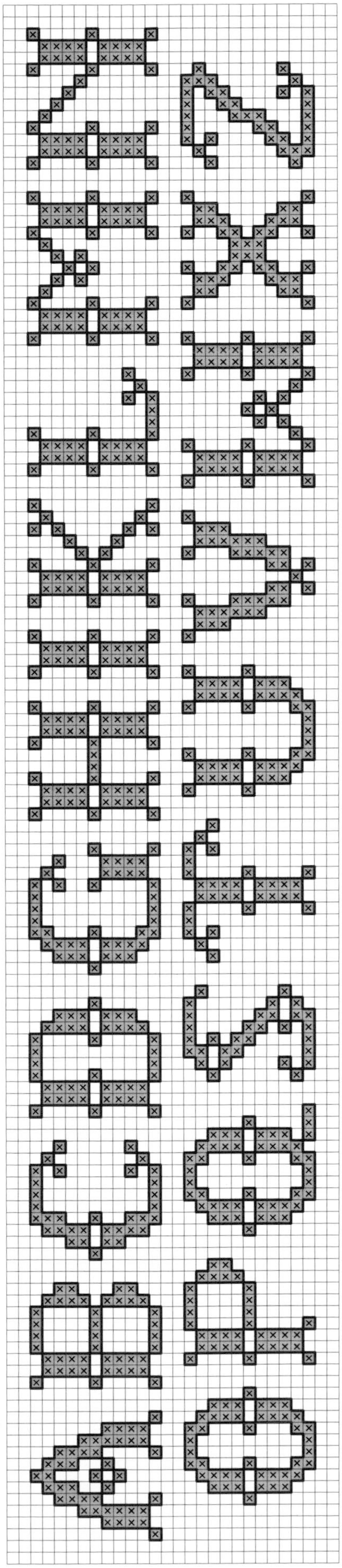

Let It Snow Alphabet

## Let It Snow Stockings

*The chart and key are on pages 64–66.*

### Supplies

*For the large stocking*
27×18" piece of 14-count white Aida cloth
20×15" piece of fusible fleece
1 yard of 45"-wide red-and-white check fabric
1¼ yard of ¼"-diameter cording
*For each small stocking*
18×15" piece of 28-count pewter Jobelan fabric
15×12" piece of fusible fleece
¾ yard of 45"-wide blue-print cotton fabric
¾ yard of ⅛"-diameter cording
*For all stockings*
Graph paper; pencil
Erasable fabric marker
Cotton embroidery floss
Matching sewing thread

### Stitches

Use the alphabet to chart the desired name on graph paper, separating the letters with two squares.

For the large stocking, center and stitch the chart on the fabric. Use three plies of floss unless otherwise specified in the key.

For a small stocking, enlarge the pattern, *opposite*. Use the marker to trace the stocking pattern onto the fabric. Beginning four threads from the top of the outline, stitch the left portion of the border to fill the outline, using three plies of floss over two threads unless otherwise specified. Use the chart, *opposite,* to stitch the toe. Referring to the photo on *page 53,* center and stitch one snow person.

### Assembly

For the large stocking, center and fuse the fleece to the back of the stitched piece following the manufacturer's instructions. Use the erasable marker to draw the stocking outline as indicated by the dashed line on the chart. Cut out the stocking ½" beyond the marked line.

Use the stocking as a pattern to cut a matching back and two lining pieces from the red-and-white check fabric. Cut a 1⅝×5" hanging strip from the red fabric. Also bias-cut and piece strips to make a 1⅝×43" piping strip from the red fabric.

For a small stocking, fuse the fleece to the back of the stitched piece following the manufacturer's instructions. Cut out the stocking ½" beyond the marked line. Use the stocking as a pattern to cut a matching back and two lining pieces from the blue-print fabric. Also cut a ¾×4" hanging strip and a 1¼×27" piping strip from the blue-print fabric.

For all stockings, center the cording lengthwise on the wrong side of the piping strip. Fold the fabric around the cording with the raw edges together. Use a zipper foot to sew through both layers close to the cording.

Baste the piping around the sides and foot of the stocking front with the raw edges even. With right sides together, sew the stocking front to the back along the basting lines, leaving the top edge open.

Press the long edges of the hanging strip under ¼", fold in half lengthwise, and topstitch. Fold the strip in half to form a loop. Tack the ends inside the top right side of the stocking.

With right sides together, sew the stocking lining together, leaving the top edge open and an opening in the foot; *do not* turn. Slip the stocking inside the lining. Stitch the stocking to the lining at the top edges with right sides together; turn. Slip-stitch the opening closed. Tuck the lining into the stocking, and press carefully.

## Pocket Pal Dolls

*The charts and keys are on pages 68–69.*

### Supplies

*For each doll*
2—10" squares of 14-count white Aida cloth
5" square of fusible fleece
Cotton embroidery floss
Polyester fiberfill
Plastic pellets
Matching sewing thread

### Stitches

Center and stitch each chart on one square of fabric. Use three plies of floss unless otherwise specified.

*Continued*

**Assembly**

Press the stitched piece from the back. Center and fuse the fleece to the back of the stitched piece following the manufacturer's instructions. Machine-baste one square beyond the outermost edges of the stitching, keeping the curves smooth. Center the stitched piece atop the remaining unstitched piece of Aida cloth, right sides together; pin. Sew the two pieces together along the basting line, leaving the bottom edge open for turning. Trim the seam allowances to ¼". Clip curves; turn right side out. Using tiny pieces of fiberfill, stuff the small curved areas of the head. Fill remainder of doll with plastic pellets and hand-sew the opening closed.

*Pocket Pals*

| Anchor | | DMC | |
|---|---|---|---|
| 002 | ⊡ | 000 | White |
| 897 | ▲ | 221 | Deep shell pink |
| 403 | ■ | 310 | Black |
| 218 | ⧗ | 319 | Dark pistachio |
| 1025 | ▯ | 347 | Salmon |
| 214 | ✱ | 368 | Light pistachio |
| 301 | ▷ | 744 | Yellow |
| 043 | ⊠ | 815 | Garnet |
| 390 | ◎ | 822 | Beige-gray |
| 1035 | ◆ | 930 | Dark antique blue |
| 1033 | ⊕ | 932 | True antique blue |
| 382 | ● | 3371 | Black-brown |
| 1050 | ⊙ | 3781 | Dark mocha |

BACKSTITCH

| | | | |
|---|---|---|---|
| 002 | ⁄ | 000 | White – boy's shoelaces (2X) and boy's jeans (1X) |
| 382 | ⁄ | 3371 | Black-brown – all other stitches (1X) |

Light Skin Tones

| Anchor | | DMC | |
|---|---|---|---|
| 914 | ◪ | 407 | Medium cocoa – inside mouth |
| 1012 | ⊟ | 754 | Peach |
| 882 | ⧄ | 758 | Light terra-cotta – cheeks |

BACKSTITCH

| | | | |
|---|---|---|---|
| 914 | ⁄ | 407 | Medium cocoa – nose (1X) |
| 896 | ⁄ | 3721 | Dark shell pink – lips (2X) |

FRENCH KNOT

| | | | |
|---|---|---|---|
| 914 | • | 407 | Medium cocoa – freckles and dimples (1X wrapped once) |

Dark Skin Tones

| Anchor | | DMC | |
|---|---|---|---|
| 896 | ◪ | 3721 | Dark shell pink – inside mouth |
| 1007 | ⊟ | 3772 | Dark cocoa |
| 1013 | ⧄ | 3778 | True terra-cotta – cheeks |

BACKSTITCH

| | | | |
|---|---|---|---|
| 043 | ⁄ | 815 | Garnet – lips (2X) |
| 1050 | ⁄ | 3781 | Dark mocha – nose (1X) |

FRENCH KNOT

| | | | |
|---|---|---|---|
| 1050 | • | 3781 | Dark mocha – freckles and dimples (1X wrapped once) |

*Boy Pocket Pal*

*Girl Pocket Pal*

Blonde Hair

| Anchor | | DMC | |
|---|---|---|---|
| 891 | ⊞ | 676 | Light old gold |
| 886 | ▽ | 677 | Pale old gold |

BACKSTITCH

| | | | |
|---|---|---|---|
| 1050 | / | 3781 | Dark mocha – eyebrows (1X) |

Red Hair

| | | | |
|---|---|---|---|
| 352 | ⊞ | 300 | Mahogany |
| 1015 | ▽ | 918 | Red-copper |

BACKSTITCH

| | | | |
|---|---|---|---|
| 352 | / | 300 | Mahogany – eyebrows (1X) |

Black Hair

| | | | |
|---|---|---|---|
| 403 | ⊞ | 310 | Black |
| 1041 | ▽ | 844 | Beaver gray |

BACKSTITCH

| | | | |
|---|---|---|---|
| 382 | / | 3371 | Black-brown – eyebrows (1X) |

Brown Hair

| | | | |
|---|---|---|---|
| 905 | ⊞ | 3021 | Brown-gray |
| 1050 | ▽ | 3781 | Dark mocha |

BACKSTITCH

| | | | |
|---|---|---|---|
| 382 | / | 3371 | Black-brown – eyebrows (1X) |

Eye Color

| Anchor | | DMC | |
|---|---|---|---|
| 218 | ♥ | 319 | Dark pistachio – green eyes |
| 1035 | ♥ | 930 | Dark antique blue – blue eyes |
| 905 | ♥ | 3021 | Brown-gray – brown eyes |
| 382 | ♥ | 3371 | Black-brown – dark brown eyes |

Light Fur

| Anchor | | DMC | |
|---|---|---|---|
| 832 | ⊘ | 612 | Medium drab brown |
| 831 | △ | 613 | Light drab brown |
| 882 | / | 758 | Light terra-cotta |

Dark Fur

| | | | |
|---|---|---|---|
| 903 | △ | 3032 | Medium mocha |
| 1007 | / | 3772 | Dark cocoa |
| 1050 | ⊘ | 3781 | Dark mocha |

***Boy and Girl***
***Stitch count:*** *55 high x 45 wide*
***Finished design sizes:***
*14-count fabric – 3⅞ x 3¼ inches*
*18-count fabric – 3 x 2½ inches*

***Girl Bear***
***Stitch count:*** *57 high x 45 wide*
***Finished design sizes:***
*14-count fabric – 4 x 3¼ inches*
*18-count fabric – 3⅛ x 2½ inches*

***Boy Bear***
***Stitch count:*** *56 high x 45 wide*
***Finished design sizes:***
*14-count fabric – 4 x 3¼ inches*
*18-count fabric – 3⅛ x 2½ inches*

*Boy Bear Pocket Pal*

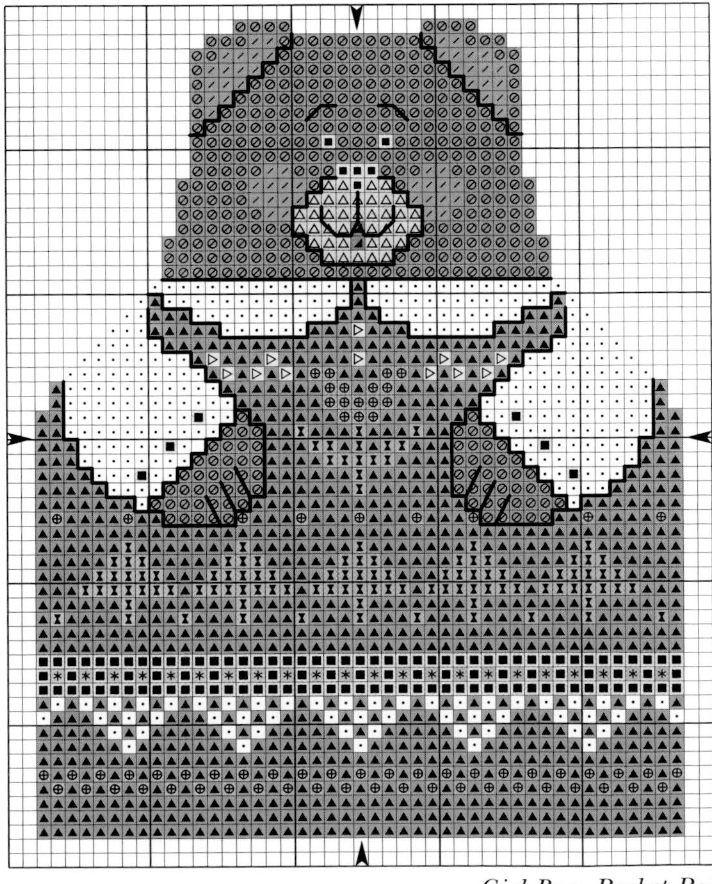

*Girl Bear Pocket Pal*

# All That

# Glitters

*From sparkling snowflakes to twinkling lights, every aspect of Christmas glows. This special collection of ornaments and trims is enhanced with glistening metallic threads to shine like the radiance of the holidays.*

The benevolence of the saint from whom he originated shines in the face of this Old World Santa. Stitched on 32-count natural linen, his is a perfect portrait to frame and display in a holiday home. The intense detail of the chart adapts well to 10-count linen that's as easy to stitch as Aida cloth. It carries an easy elegance when finished as a pillow, surrounded by velveteen and golden trims.

*Design: Carol Emmer*

■

If you haven't tried Hardanger, this spectacular ornament, *left,* is the place to start. The lacy pattern, formed by basic Hardanger stitches, surrounds a delicate sprig of holly.

Horse-pulled sleighs are no longer necessary for holiday travel, but their cheery bells still brighten the Christmas season as a jingle bell ornament, *below,* to sparkle on your tree.

Madonna and Child—the essence of Christmas—are surrounded by golden halos and glittering braid. Stitch this dainty ornament on 14-count celadon Aida cloth and accent it with gold thread.

*Designs: Hardanger, Emie Bishop;*
*jingle bells, Barbara Sestok;*
*Madonna and Child, Ursula Michael*

■

Is there a more appropriate figure for a tree skirt than stately Father Christmas, his pack overflowing with Christmas toys? The prefinished 10-count Tilla tree skirt means easy stitching. For a framed piece, omit the garland that extends around the skirt. And remember to make your packages special by stitching selected toys for gift tags.

*Design: Barbara Sestok*

The natural shimmer of peacock feathers and the warmth of candlelight brighten a holiday home. A malachite-finish tray, *opposite,* complements the rich colors and metallic threads of the rose and feather wreath.

Light the way to Christmas cheer with a holly and candle ornament, *above,* encircled with shiny gold and red braids.

*Designs: Wreath, Ursula Michael; ornament, Barbara Sestok*

Brass instruments herald the good news of Christmas, and their warm patina reflects the opulence of the season. Golden pears and metallic lace set off the elegant French horn on this ornament.

*Design: Diana Thomas*

## Old World Santa

### Supplies

*9" square of 32-count natural brown linen*
*Cotton embroidery floss*
*Kreinik blending filament*
*Mill Hill seed beads*
*Desired frame*

### Stitches

Center and stitch the chart using two plies over two threads unless otherwise specified. Press from the back.

## Old World Santa Pillow

### Supplies

*15×18" piece of 10-count navy Betsy Ross linen fabric*
*Cotton embroidery floss*
*Kreinik blending filament*
*7½×8¼" piece of navy cotton fabric*
*⅜ yard of 45"-wide red velveteen fabric*
*1 yard of ½"-wide metallic gold flat braid*
*1⅜ yards of red-and-gold ⅜"-diameter sew-in cording*
*Polyester fiberfill*

### Stitches

Center and stitch the chart on the fabric using four plies over one square of the fabric. Work the blended-needle stitches using two plies of floss and two strands of filament. Use two plies of floss to work the straight stitches and the backstitches. Press the stitched piece from the back.

### Assembly

Centering the design, trim the stitched piece to measure 7½×8¼". Center the stitched piece right side up on the navy fabric; baste in place ½" from outside edges. Trim the edges even with the stitched piece.

From the red velveteen, cut two 3×8¼" side sashing strips, two 3×11½" top and bottom sashing strips, and a 11½×12¼" back. Sew all seams with right sides together using ½" seams.

Machine-sew a side sashing strip to the left and right edge of the stitched piece. Press seam allowances toward the sashing.

Sew sashing strips to the top and bottom edges in the same manner. Press the seam allowances toward the

*Continued*

*Old World Santa*

| | | |
|---|---|---|
| 9046 | ⊡ | 321 True Christmas red |
| 009 | ⧄ | 352 Coral |
| 008 | ⧍ | 353 Dark peach |
| 358 | ● | 433 Dark chestnut |
| 310 | ⊠ | 434 Medium chestnut |
| 1046 | ▽ | 435 Light chestnut |
| 1005 | # | 498 Dark Christmas red |
| 392 | ☆ | 642 Medium beige-gray |
| 830 | ⊟ | 644 Light beige-gray |
| 046 | ♡ | 666 Red |
| 882 | L | 758 Light terra-cotta |
| 390 | I | 822 Pale beige-gray |
| 897 | ♥ | 902 Garnet |
| 1034 | ⊚ | 931 Antique blue |
| 1011 | ⁚ | 948 Light peach |
| 360 | ◆ | 3031 Mocha |
| 883 | △ | 3064 Light cocoa |
| 031 | ⊞ | 3708 Light watermelon |
| 1009 | ∾ | 3770 Ivory |
| 1007 | ◙ | 3772 Dark cocoa |
| 035 | ⁘ | 3801 Deep watermelon |

BLENDED NEEDLE

| | | |
|---|---|---|
| 890 | ◇ | 729 Old gold (1X) and 002 Kreinik Gold blending filament (1X) |

BACKSTITCH (1X)

| | | |
|---|---|---|
| 5975 | / | 356 Terra-cotta – nose |
| 217 | / | 367 Pistachio – border |
| 360 | / | 3031 Mocha – eyes |

STRAIGHT STITCH (1X)

| | | |
|---|---|---|
| 002 | / | 000 White – eye brows |

BLENDED-NEEDLE FRENCH KNOT

| | | |
|---|---|---|
| 890 | ● | 729 Old gold (2X) and 002 Kreinik Gold blending filament (2X wrapped once) – Santa pillow |

MILL HILL BEADS

● 00557 Gold seed beads – Santa ornament

***Ornament stitch count:*** *64 high x 46 wide*

***Ornament finished design sizes:***
*32-count fabric – 4 x 2⅞ inches*
*28-count fabric – 4½ x 3¼ inches*
*36-count fabric – 3½ x 2½ inches*

***Pillow stitch count:*** *64 high x 46 wide*

***Pillow finished design sizes:***
*10-count fabric – 6⅜ x 4⅔ inches*
*12-count fabric – 5⅓ x 3¾ inches*
*8-count fabric – 8 x 5¾ inches*

sashing. Topstitch the gold braid to sashing strips, aligning the straight edge of braid with the inside edge of sashing strips.

Baste the cording around the pillow front. Sew the pillow front and the pillow back together, leaving an opening for turning. Trim the seams, clip the corners, and turn right side out. Press the pillow carefully. Stuff the pillow firmly with fiberfill; slip-stitch the opening closed.

## Holly and Hardanger Ornament

### Supplies

*6" square of 32-count cream Belfast linen*
*Cotton embroidery floss*
*#8 and #12 pearl cotton*
*Mill Hill seed beads*

### Stitches

Center and stitch the chart on the fabric. Use two plies of floss to work the cross-stitches over two threads of fabric. Use one strand of pearl cotton to work the remaining stitches referring to the diagrams *below*. For the Algerian eyelets, give each stitch a gentle tug to create a small opening.

Referring to the diagrams *below,* cut and remove threads. Then use a 30" length of pearl cotton to work the needleweaving.

Trim the fabric around the outside edge of the ornament close to the stitching. Attach the seed beads using two plies of floss. Place the stitchery facedown on a soft towel and press from the back.

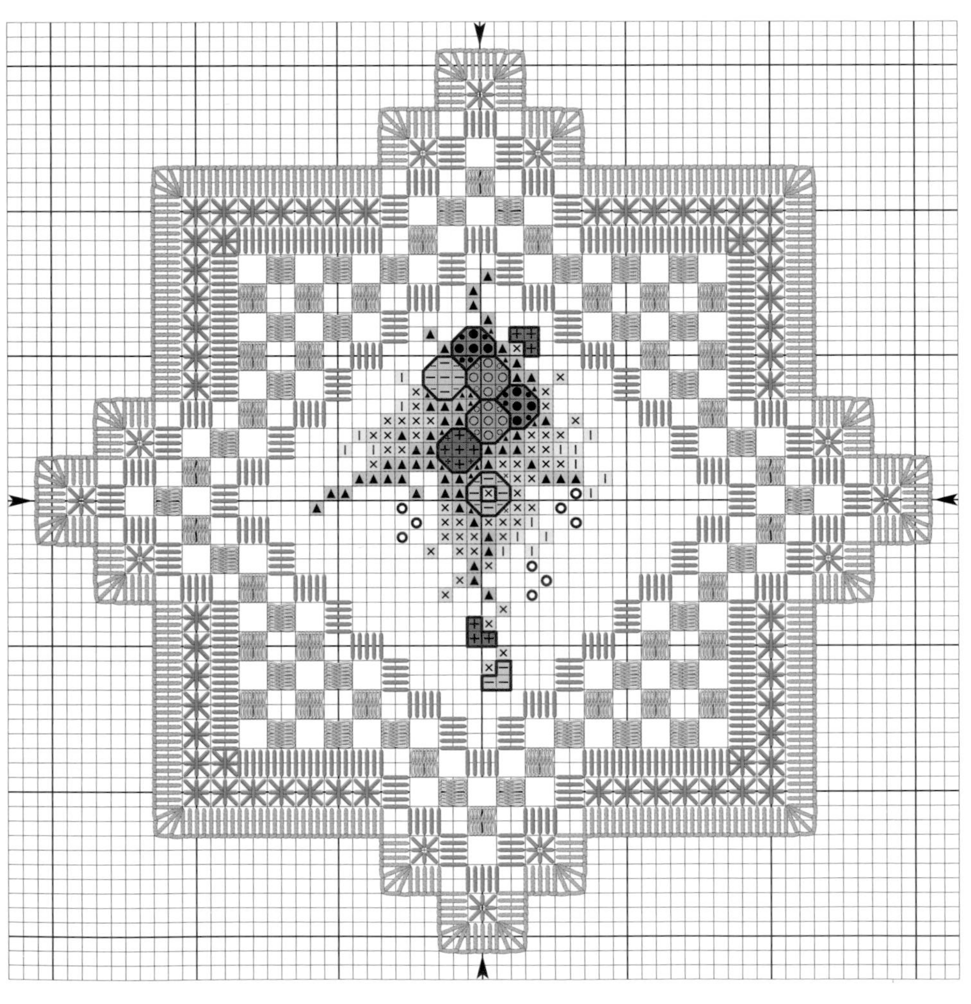

*Holly and Hardanger Ornament*

| Anchor | | DMC |
|---|---|---|
| 1005 | ⊡ | 498 Christmas red |
| 043 | ● | 815 Garnet |
| 035 | + | 891 Dark carnation |
| 027 | – | 894 Pale carnation |
| 1044 | ▲ | 895 Dark hunter green |
| 267 | × | 3346 Light hunter green |
| 266 | I | 3347 Yellow-green |

BACKSTITCH
043 / 815 Garnet – berries and buds (1X)
KLOSTER BLOCK
Ecru #8 pearl cotton
BUTTONHOLE STITCH
Ecru #8 pearl cotton
SMYRNA CROSS-STITCH (8 legs over 4)
Ecru #12 pearl cotton
ALGERIAN EYELET (8 legs over 4)
Ecru #12 pearl cotton
NEEDLEWEAVING
Ecru #12 pearl cotton
MILL HILL BEADS
○ 03003 Antique cranberry seed beads

***Stitch count:*** *62 high x 62 wide*

***Finished design sizes:***
*32-count fabric – 3⅞ x 3⅞ inches*
*28-count fabric – 4⅜ x 4⅜ inches*
*36-count fabric – 3½ x 3½ inches*

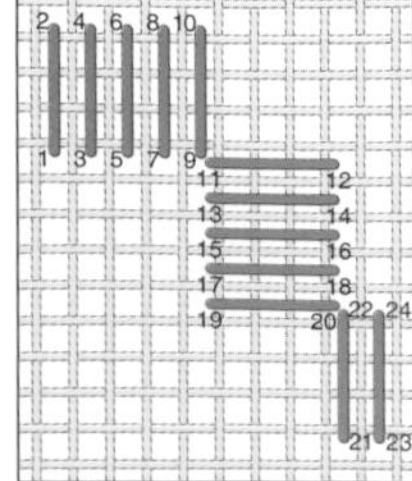


*Kloster Blocks*

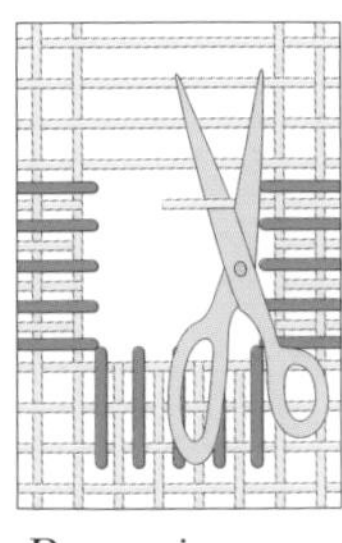

*Removing Threads*

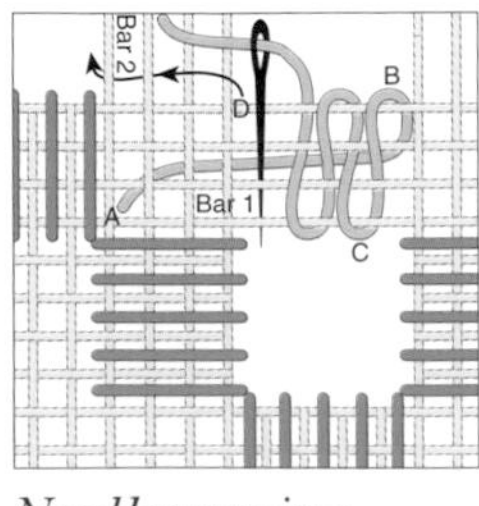


*Needleweaving*

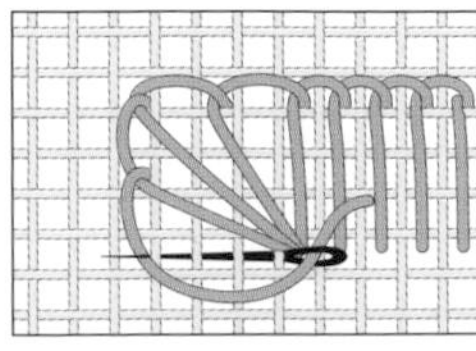

*Buttonhole Stitch*

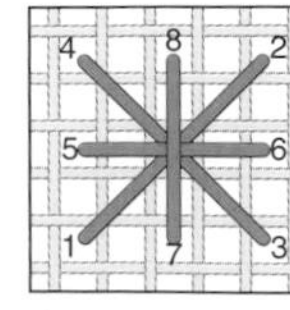


*Smyrna Cross-Stitch*

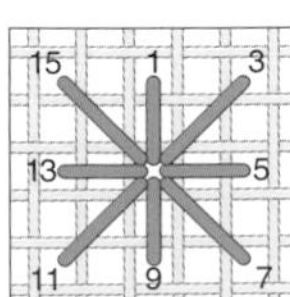


*Algerian Eyelet*

# Jingle Bell Ornament

## Supplies

*10×12" piece of 28-count glass blue Monaco fabric*
*Cotton embroidery floss*
*Erasable fabric marker*
*Tracing paper*
*4½×6" piece of self-stick mounting board with foam*
*4½×6" piece of light blue felt*
*½ yard of ⅜"-wide metallic gold-and-green flat trim*
*6" length of Kreinik 002 Gold #8 braid*
*Crafts glue*

## Stitches

Center and stitch the chart on the fabric using three plies of floss over two threads unless otherwise specified. Press carefully from the back.

## Assembly

Use the erasable marker to draw an outline around the stitched area of the design as indicated by the dashed line on the chart; *do not* cut out. Place the tracing paper over the fabric and trace the ornament outline. Cut out the paper pattern. Use the pattern to cut matching shapes from the mounting board and the felt.

Peel the protective paper from the mounting board. Center the foam side on the back of the stitchery and press to stick. Trim the excess fabric ½" beyond the edge of the board. Fold the edge of the fabric to the back and glue in place.

Position and glue the trim around the edge of the ornament, overlapping the ends at the bottom center and trimming the excess. For the hanger, fold the braid in half to form a loop. Glue the braid ends to the top center of the ornament back. Glue the felt to the back of the ornament.

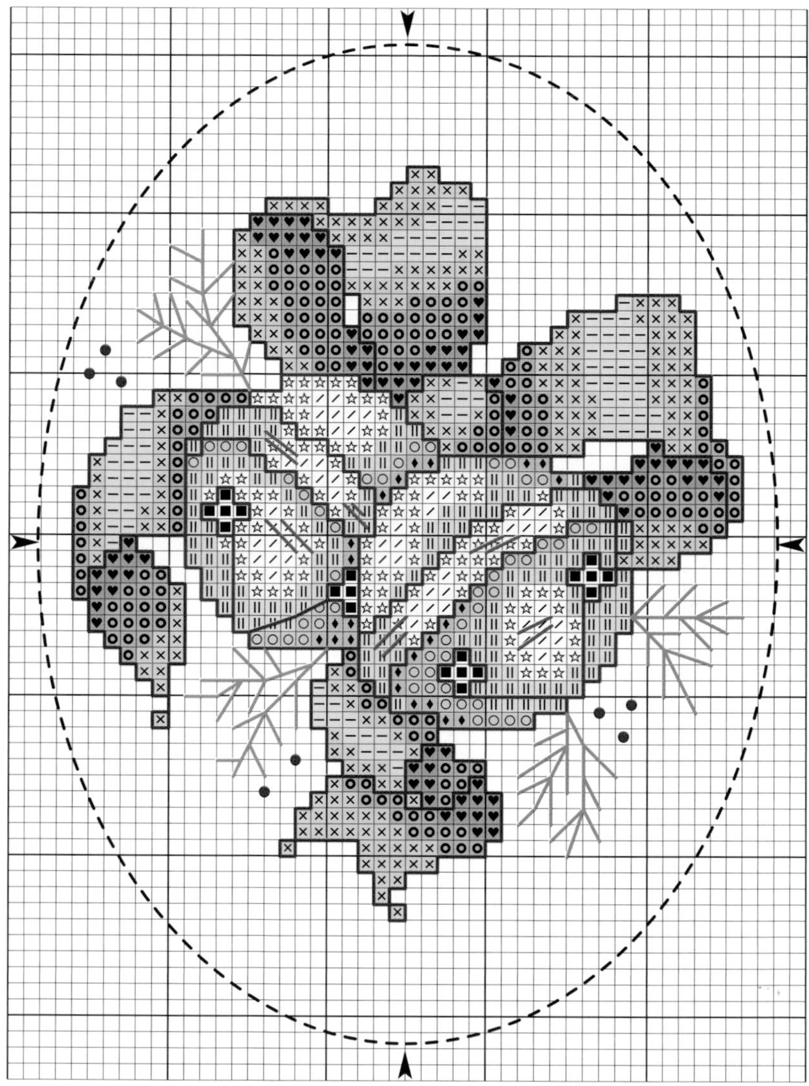

*Jingle Bell Ornament*

| Anchor | | DMC |
|---|---|---|
| 1025 | ⊙ | 347 Salmon |
| 010 | ⊠ | 351 Coral |
| 358 | ♦ | 433 Dark chestnut |
| 1046 | ○ | 435 Light chestnut |
| 305 | ☆ | 725 Topaz |
| 307 | ǁ | 783 Christmas gold |
| 1005 | ♥ | 816 Light garnet |
| 360 | ■ | 3031 Mocha |
| 292 | ⁄ | 3078 Lemon |
| 328 | ⊟ | 3341 Melon |

STRAIGHT STITCH (1X)
275 ⁄ 746 Off-white – jingle bell detail

BACKSTITCH (1X)
897 ⁄ 902 Deep garnet – ribbon
360 ⁄ 3031 Mocha – jingle bells

BLENDED-NEEDLE BACKSTITCH
923 ⁄ 699 Christmas green (1X) and
204 913 Nile green (1X) – pine greens

FRENCH KNOT
010 ● 351 Coral – holly berries (1X wrapped once)

***Stitch count:*** *47 high x 42 wide*

***Finished design sizes:***
*28-count fabric – 3⅓ x 3 inches*
*32-count fabric – 2⅞ x 2⅝ inches*
*36-count fabric – 2⅔ x 2⅓ inches*

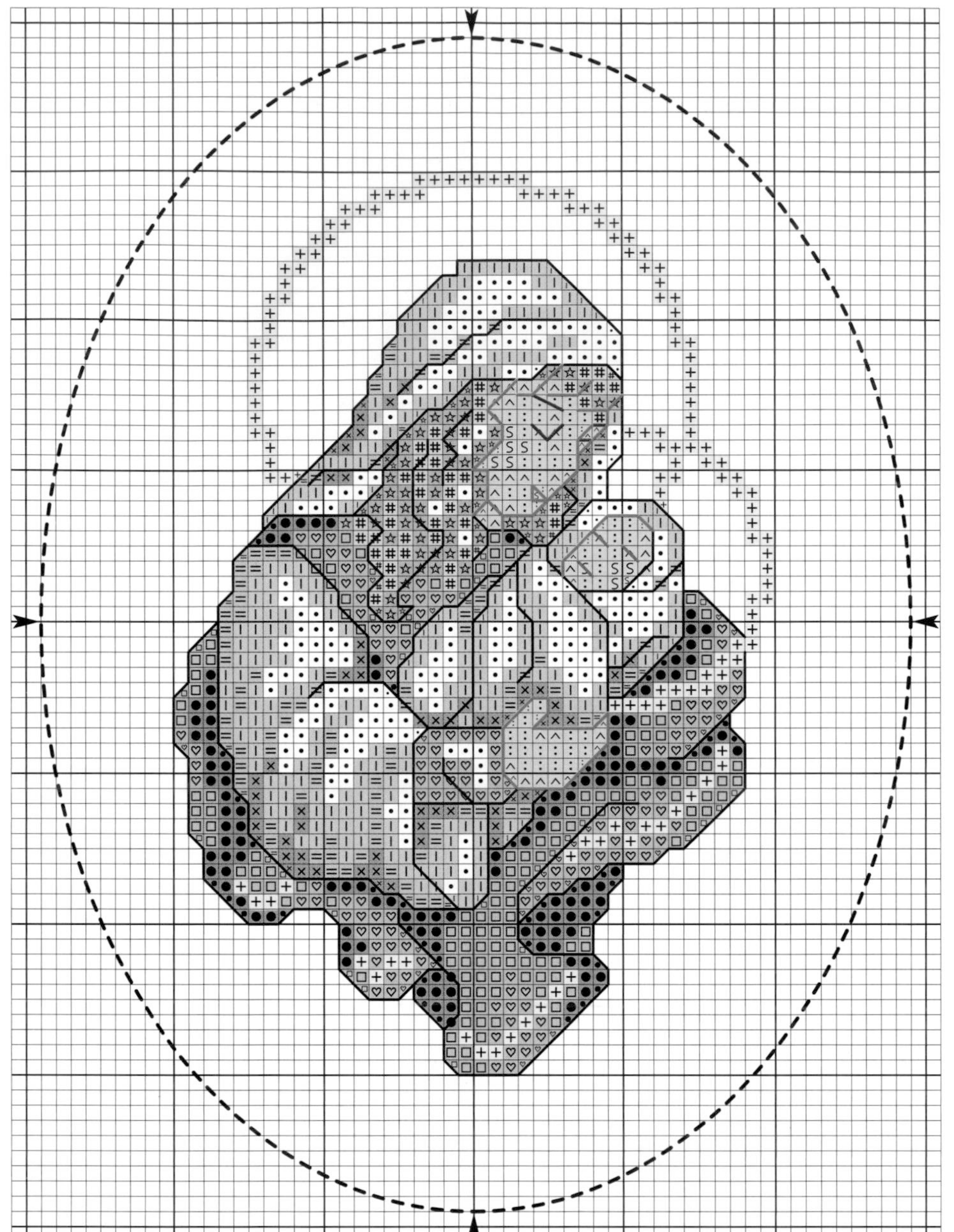

### *Madonna and Child Ornament*

| Anchor | DMC |
|---|---|
| 002 | 000 White |
| 897 | 221 Deep shell pink |
| 895 | 223 Medium shell pink |
| 117 | 341 Light periwinkle |
| 310 | 434 Chestnut |
| 1045 | 436 Tan |
| 176 | 793 Cornflower blue |
| 881 | 945 Dark ivory |
| 1010 | 951 Medium ivory |
| 1027 | 3722 True shell pink |
| 120 | 3747 Pale periwinkle |
| 868 | 3779 Terra-cotta |
| | 5282 Metallic gold |
| BACKSTITCH (1X) | |
| 310 | 434 Chestnut – baby eyes, mouth |
| 359 | 801 Medium coffee brown – Madonna eyes, eyebrows |
| 360 | 898 Dark coffee brown – all other stitches |
| 883 | 3064 Cocoa – hand and faces |

***Stitch count:** 60 high x 40 wide*

***Finished design sizes:***
*14-count fabric – 4¼ x 2⅞ inches*
*16-count fabric – 3¾ x 2½ inches*
*18-count fabric – 3⅓ x 2¼ inches*

## Madonna and Child Ornament

### Supplies

*10×12" piece of 14-count moss/celadon Aida cloth*
*Cotton embroidery floss*
*DMC metallic embroidery floss*
*Tracing paper*
*Erasable fabric marker*
*6×8" piece of self-stick mounting board with foam*
*¾ yard of ⅛"-diameter metallic gold twisted cord*
*Crafts glue*
*6×8" piece of white felt*

### Stitches

Center and stitch the chart using three plies of floss unless otherwise specified. Press from the back.

### Assembly

Use the erasable marker to draw an outline around the stitched area of the design as indicated by the dashed line on the chart; *do not* cut out. Place the tracing paper over the fabric and trace the ornament outline. Cut out the paper pattern. Use the paper pattern to cut matching shapes from the mounting board and the felt.

Peel the protective paper from the mounting board. Center the foam side on the back of the stitchery and press to stick. Trim the excess fabric ½" beyond the edge of the board. Fold the edge of the fabric to the back and glue in place.

Cut an 18" length of gold cord. Position and glue the cord around the edge of the ornament, overlapping the ends at the bottom center and trimming the excess. For the hanger, fold the remaining cord in half to form a loop. Glue the cord ends to the top center of the ornament back. Glue the felt to the back of the ornament.

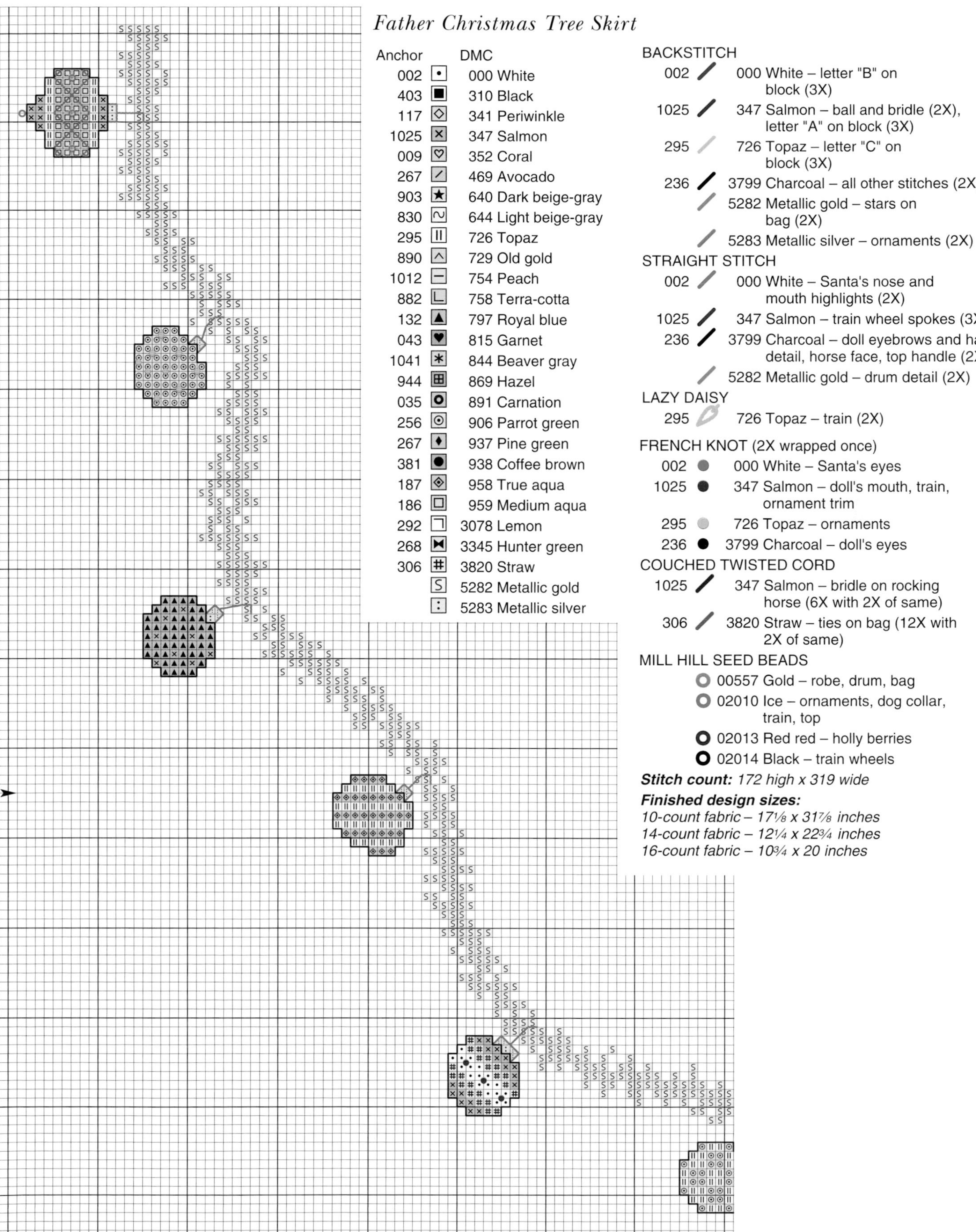

## *Father Christmas Tree Skirt*

| Anchor | DMC |
|---|---|
| 002 | 000 White |
| 403 | 310 Black |
| 117 | 341 Periwinkle |
| 1025 | 347 Salmon |
| 009 | 352 Coral |
| 267 | 469 Avocado |
| 903 | 640 Dark beige-gray |
| 830 | 644 Light beige-gray |
| 295 | 726 Topaz |
| 890 | 729 Old gold |
| 1012 | 754 Peach |
| 882 | 758 Terra-cotta |
| 132 | 797 Royal blue |
| 043 | 815 Garnet |
| 1041 | 844 Beaver gray |
| 944 | 869 Hazel |
| 035 | 891 Carnation |
| 256 | 906 Parrot green |
| 267 | 937 Pine green |
| 381 | 938 Coffee brown |
| 187 | 958 True aqua |
| 186 | 959 Medium aqua |
| 292 | 3078 Lemon |
| 268 | 3345 Hunter green |
| 306 | 3820 Straw |
| | 5282 Metallic gold |
| | 5283 Metallic silver |

BACKSTITCH
002 000 White – letter "B" on block (3X)
1025 347 Salmon – ball and bridle (2X), letter "A" on block (3X)
295 726 Topaz – letter "C" on block (3X)
236 3799 Charcoal – all other stitches (2X)
5282 Metallic gold – stars on bag (2X)
5283 Metallic silver – ornaments (2X)

STRAIGHT STITCH
002 000 White – Santa's nose and mouth highlights (2X)
1025 347 Salmon – train wheel spokes (3X)
236 3799 Charcoal – doll eyebrows and hat detail, horse face, top handle (2X)
5282 Metallic gold – drum detail (2X)

LAZY DAISY
295 726 Topaz – train (2X)

FRENCH KNOT (2X wrapped once)
002 000 White – Santa's eyes
1025 347 Salmon – doll's mouth, train, ornament trim
295 726 Topaz – ornaments
236 3799 Charcoal – doll's eyes

COUCHED TWISTED CORD
1025 347 Salmon – bridle on rocking horse (6X with 2X of same)
306 3820 Straw – ties on bag (12X with 2X of same)

MILL HILL SEED BEADS
00557 Gold – robe, drum, bag
02010 Ice – ornaments, dog collar, train, top
02013 Red red – holly berries
02014 Black – train wheels

***Stitch count:*** *172 high x 319 wide*

***Finished design sizes:***
*10-count fabric – 17⅛ x 31⅞ inches*
*14-count fabric – 12¼ x 22¾ inches*
*16-count fabric – 10¾ x 20 inches*

*Father Christmas Tree Skirt (left side)*

*Father Christmas Tree Skirt (center)*

## Father Christmas Tree Skirt

*The chart and key begin on page 85.*

### Supplies

*Purchased 32"-diameter 10-count cream-and-gold Tilla tree skirt*
*Cotton embroidery floss*
*DMC metallic floss*
*1 additional skein each of white, salmon (DMC 347), royal blue (797), parrot green (906), charcoal (3799), and metallic gold (5282)*
*Mill Hill seed beads*

### Stitches

Find the vertical center of the chart and the tree skirt. Count six squares up from the fringed edge; begin stitching there. Use four plies of floss to work the cross-stitches unless otherwise specified in the key.

For the bridle, cut three 20" plies of salmon floss (DMC 347). Combine into a single strand. Secure one end of the strand and twist until it's tightly wound. Holding the ends, fold the strand in half as the two halves twist around each other. Knot one end of the cord; thread the other end into a large tapestry needle. Insert the needle into the back of the fabric at the position marked on the chart. Bring the twisted cord across the front of the fabric to the other position marked on the horse. Refer to the diagram and use two plies of matching floss to work couching stitches over the cord.

For the bag ties, cut two 20" six-ply strands of straw floss (DMC 3820). Twist and fold one strand as directed for the bridle, *above*. Thread one end into a large tapestry needle. Securing the tail, insert the needle into the back of the fabric at the position marked on the chart and pull through. Remove the needle, tie a knot ½" from the end, and trim the end to ¼". Twist the remaining strand of floss, attaching it at the other side of the bag in the same manner. Tie the cord ends in a knot at the center of the bag. Use matching floss to loosely couch the ties to the bag.

Attach the seed beads using two plies of floss. Press the skirt carefully from the back.

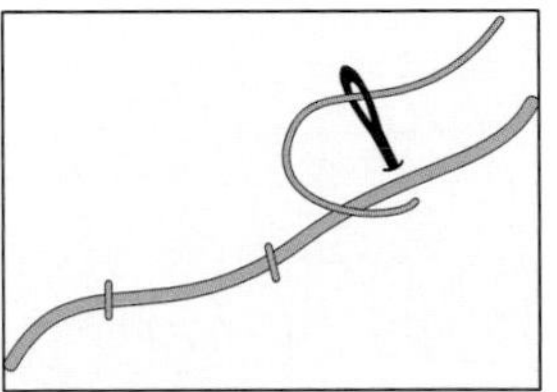

*Couching*

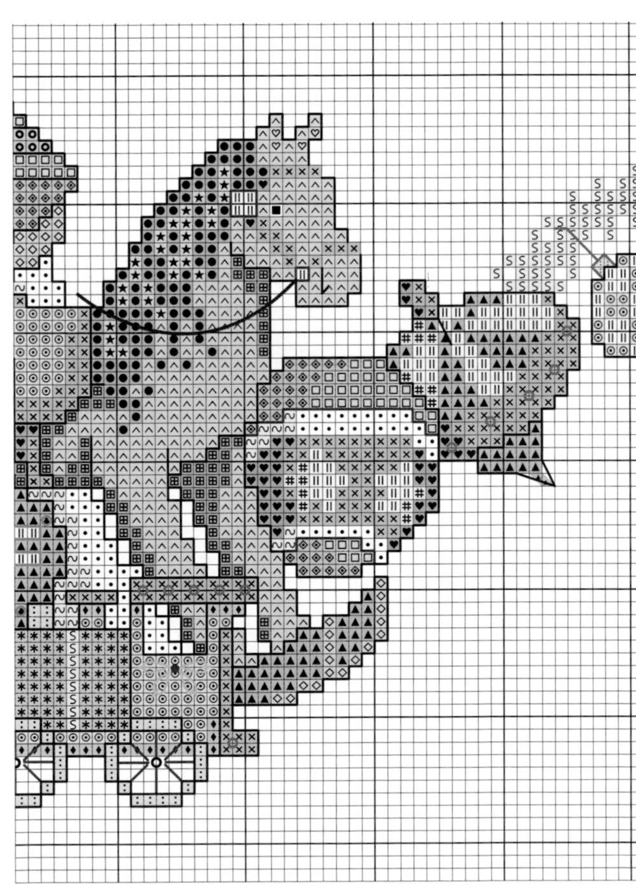

## Toy Package Ties

*The chart and key begin on page 85.*

### Supplies

*3" squares of white perforated paper*
*Cotton embroidery floss*
*DMC metallic floss*
*Crafts glue*
*White vellum paper*
*Decorative edge scissors (optional)*
*Paper punch*
*6" lengths of narrow ribbon*

### Stitches

Center and stitch any of the toys or ornaments from the Father Christmas chart on a square of perforated paper using two plies of floss unless otherwise specified.

### Assembly

Cut out the motif one square beyond the stitching. Cut a 2½×5" vellum rectangle and fold it in half. Trim edges with decorative edge scissors, if desired. Glue the stitched piece to the front of the card. Punch a hole near the folded edge and thread the ribbon through it.

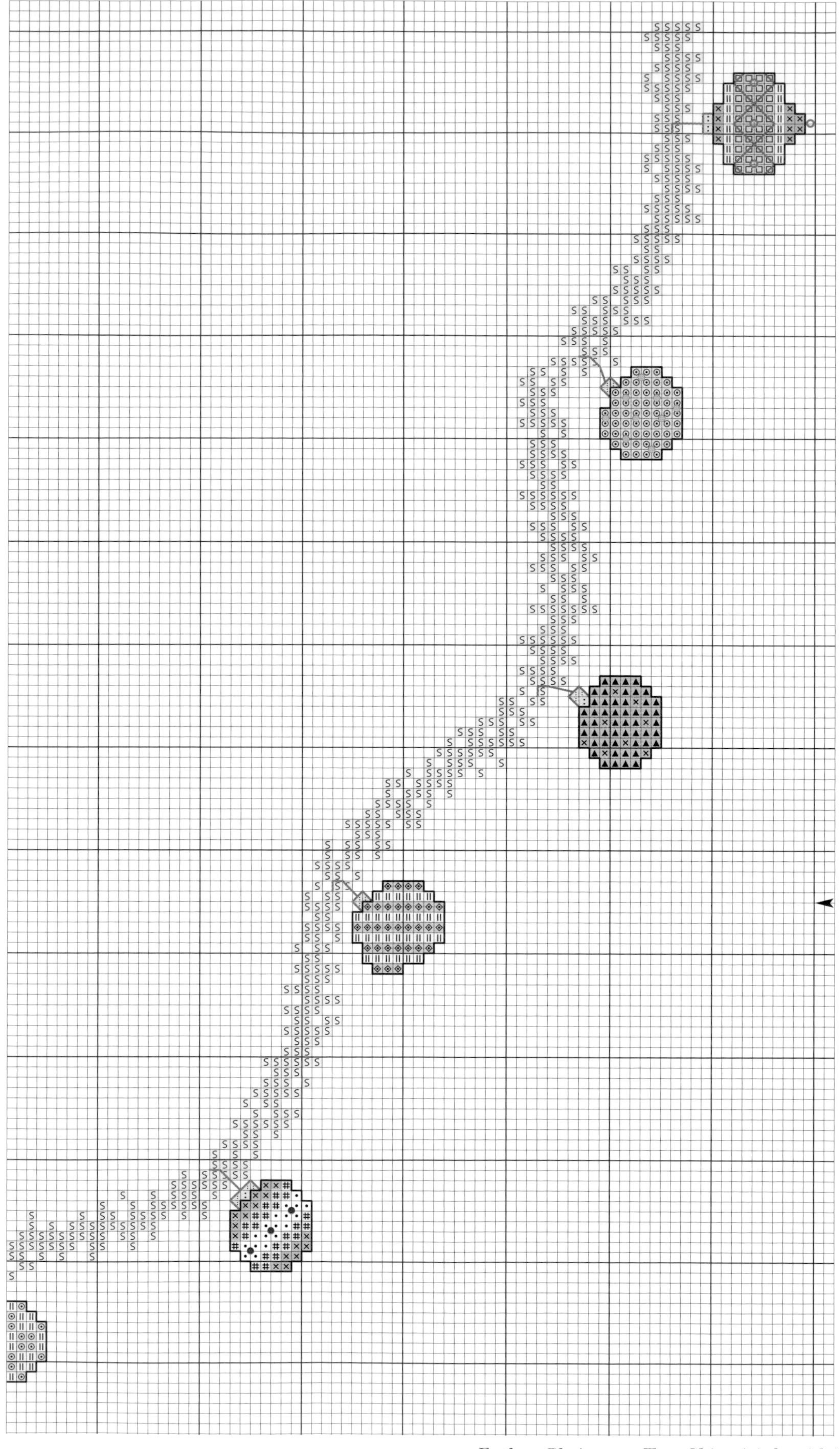

*Father Christmas Tree Skirt (right side)*

## Winter Holiday Wreath

### Supplies

*20" square of 28-count water lily linen*
*Cotton embroidery floss*
*Kreinik metallic braid*
*Purchased malachite-green 9½"-square tray with an 8¾"-square design area*
*Spray adhesive*
*9½" square of fleece*
*Crafts glue or tape*

### Stitches

Center and stitch the chart using three plies of floss over two threads unless otherwise specified. Press from the back.

### Assembly

Spray the mounting board from the tray lightly with the adhesive and position the fleece on top. Center the wrong side of the stitched piece over the fleece-covered board; glue or tape the fabric edges to the back. Insert the design into the tray and reassemble following the manufacturer's instructions.

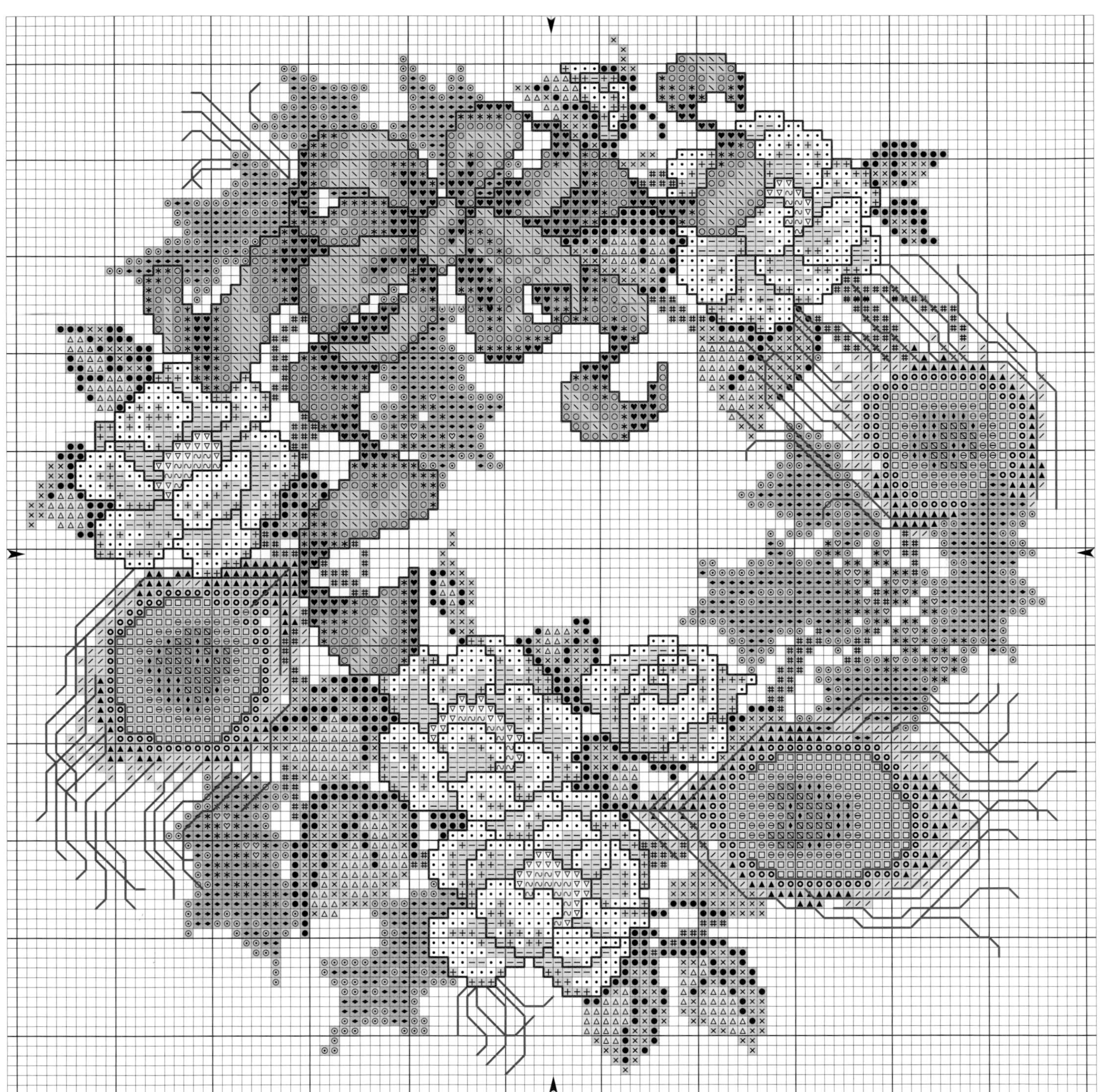

*Winter Holiday Wreath*

| Anchor | | DMC |
|---|---|---|
| 002 | • | 000 White |
| 218 | ● | 319 Dark pistachio |
| 215 | ⊠ | 320 True pistachio |
| 214 | △ | 368 Light pistachio |
| 266 | ∾ | 471 Avocado |
| 1005 | ♥ | 498 Christmas red |
| 683 | ◆ | 500 Deep blue-green |
| 877 | ⊙ | 502 Medium blue-green |
| 875 | ⁄ | 503 True blue-green |
| 046 | ✱ | 666 Red |
| 295 | ▽ | 726 Topaz |
| 133 | ⧅ | 796 Royal blue |
| 379 | # | 840 Beige-brown |
| 050 | ♡ | 957 Geranium |
| 261 | □ | 3053 Gray-green |
| 035 | ○ | 3705 Dark watermelon |
| 033 | ⧵ | 3706 Medium watermelon |
| 1020 | − | 3713 Salmon |
| | + | 007 Kreinik Pink #4 very-fine braid |
| | ◘ | 015 Kreinik Chartreuse #4 very-fine braid |
| | ♦ | 026 Kreinik Amethyst #4 very-fine braid |
| | ⊖ | 684 Kreinik Aquamarine #4 very-fine braid |
| | ▲ | 850 Kreinik Mallard #4 very-fine braid |

BACKSTITCH (1X)

| | | |
|---|---|---|
| 043 | ⁄ | 815 Garnet - flowers |
| 851 | ⁄ | 924 Gray-blue - peacock feathers |
| | ⁄ | 003V Kreinik Vintage Red #4 very-fine braid – bow |

***Stitch count:*** *107 high x 108 wide*

***Finished design sizes:***
*28-count fabric – 7⅝ x 7¾ inches*
*32-count fabric – 6⅝ x 6¾ inches*
*36-count fabric – 5⅞ x 6 inches*

## Candle and Holly Ornament

| Anchor | | DMC |
|---|---|---|
| 011 | ♥ | 350 Coral |
| 1046 | # | 435 Light chestnut |
| 830 | \ | 644 Beige-gray |
| 1040 | ∾ | 647 Beaver gray |
| 305 | ☆ | 725 Topaz |
| 275 | • | 746 Off-white |
| 307 | ⊙ | 783 Christmas gold |
| 257 | ✱ | 905 Dark parrot green |
| 255 | ○ | 907 Light parrot green |
| 292 | − | 3078 Lemon |
| 328 | + | 3341 Melon |
| 268 | ♦ | 3345 Hunter green |
| | × | 5282 Metallic gold |

BACKSTITCH (1X)

| | | |
|---|---|---|
| 358 | / | 433 Dark chestnut – candle flame |
| 360 | / | 3031 Mocha – all other stitches |
| 268 | / | 3345 Hunter green – holly leaves |

FRENCH KNOT

| | | |
|---|---|---|
| 360 | ● | 3031 Mocha – holly berries (1X wrapped once) |

***Stitch count:*** *47 high x 40 wide*

***Finished design sizes:***
*14-count fabric – 3⅓ x 2⅞ inches*
*16-count fabric – 3 x 2½ inches*
*18-count fabric – 2⅔ x 2¼ inches*

# Candle and Holly Ornament

### Supplies

*10×12" piece of 18-count basil Aida cloth*
*Cotton embroidery floss*
*DMC metallic floss*
*Erasable fabric marking pen*
*Tracing paper*
*4½×6" piece self-stick mounting board with foam*
*½ yard* each *of ¼"-diameter metallic gold cord and ⅜"-diameter red cord*
*6" length of Kreinik 002 Gold #8 braid*
*Crafts glue*
*4½×6" piece of red felt*

### Stitches

Center and stitch the chart on the fabric using two plies of floss unless otherwise specified. Press the finished stitchery carefully from the back.

### Assembly

Use the erasable marker to draw an outline around the stitched area of the design as indicated by the dashed line on the chart; *do not* cut out. Place the tracing paper over the fabric and trace the ornament outline; cut out the paper pattern. Use the pattern to cut matching shapes from the mounting board and the felt.

Peel the protective paper from the mounting board. Center the foam side on the back of the stitchery and press to stick. Trim the excess fabric ½" beyond the edge of the board. Fold the excess fabric to the back and glue in place.

Position and glue the metallic gold cord around the edge of the ornament, overlapping the ends at the bottom center and trimming the excess. For the hanger, fold the braid in half to form a loop. Glue the braid ends to the top center of the ornament back. Position and glue the red cord around the ornament behind the gold cord, overlapping the ends at the bottom and trimming the excess. Glue the felt to the ornament back.

# French Horn Ornament

### Supplies

*10" square of 36-count antique white Edinburgh linen*
*Cotton embroidery floss*
*Kreinik blending filament*
*4⅜"-diameter circle* each *of fleece, self-stick mounting board with foam, and white felt*
*Crafts glue*
*⅞ yard of ⅞"-wide gold flat lace*
*¾ yard of Kreinik 2 mm torsade cord*

### Stitches

Center and stitch the chart on the fabric using two plies of floss over two

*French Horn Ornament*

| Anchor | | DMC | |
|---|---|---|---|
| 110 | ⦶ | 208 | Lavender |
| 010 | ◇ | 351 | Coral |
| 310 | # | 434 | Chestnut |
| 1045 | D | 436 | Tan |
| 253 | – | 472 | Avocado |
| 1038 | ◎ | 519 | Dark sky blue |
| 046 | ♡ | 666 | Red |
| 323 | / | 722 | Bittersweet |
| 295 | □ | 726 | Light topaz |
| 293 | ~ | 727 | Pale topaz |
| 158 | I | 747 | Light sky blue |
| 259 | S | 772 | Loden |
| 359 | ■ | 801 | Coffee brown |
| 043 | \ | 815 | Garnet |
| 164 | ▼ | 824 | Bright blue |
| 218 | * | 890 | Pistachio |
| 209 | △ | 912 | Light emerald |
| 169 | + | 3760 | Wedgwood blue |
| 923 | ★ | 3818 | Deep emerald |
| 306 | ● | 3820 | Straw |
| 386 | · | 3823 | Yellow |

BLENDED NEEDLE

| | | | |
|---|---|---|---|
| 295 | × | 726 | Light topaz (2X) and |
| | | 002 | Kreinik gold blending filament (2X) |
| 293 | I | 727 | Pale topaz (2X) and |
| | | 002 | Kreinik gold blending filament (2X) |
| 306 | O | 3820 | Straw (2X) and |
| | | 002 | Kreinik gold blending filament (2X) |

threads of fabric unless otherwise specified. Press from the back.

**Assembly**

Peel the protective paper from the mounting board. Center the foam side on the fleece; press to stick. Trim the fleece even with the edge of the board. Trim the stitchery fabric ⅝" beyond the ornament outline on the back of the fabric. Center the fleece side of the mounting board on the back of the stitched design. Fold the excess fabric to the back and glue.

Sew a row of gathering stitches along the straight edge of lace. Pull the stitches to fit the circumference of the ornament; adjust the gathers evenly. Glue the lace to the back of the ornament. Position and glue the torsade cord around the front edge of the ornament, overlapping the ends at the bottom. Trim the excess cord; glue the ends to the back.

For the hanger, fold an 8½" piece of cord in half to make a loop. Glue the ends to the top center of the ornament back. Glue the felt to the back.

FRENCH KNOT (2X wrapped once)

359 ● 801 Coffee brown – flower centers

STRAIGHT STITCH

359 / 801 Coffee brown – flower centers (2X)

BACKSTITCH (1X)

359 / 801 Coffee brown – pear stems

382 / 3371 Black-brown – all other stitches

***Stitch count:*** *68 high x 69 wide*

***Finished design sizes:***

*36-count fabric – 3¾ x 3⅞ inches*

*28-count fabric – 4⅞ x 5 inches*

*32-count fabric – 4¼ x 4⅓ inches*

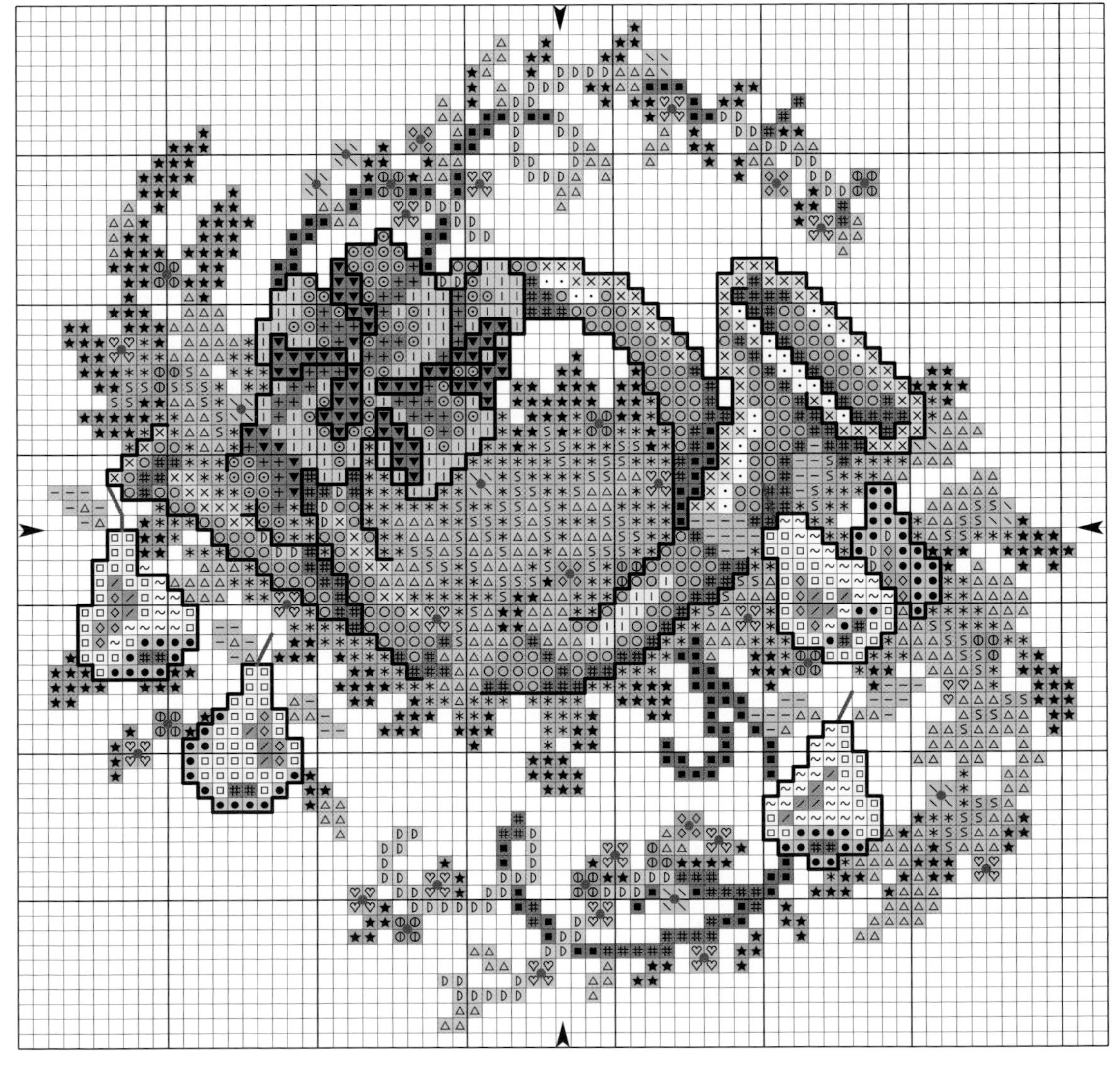

# Winter

# *Whimsy*

*Christmas is a time of laughter and good humor. To extend the merriment of the Christmas season, include some lighthearted home accessories, holiday trims, and gifts on your cross-stitching agenda.*

Ho, ho, ho, this jolly Santa, *opposite,* offers a basket or bowl of treats and decorations to all. His expressive face, stitched on 14-count Aida, tops an easily sewn velvet and fur suit.

Tweet, tweet, tweet—a little birdie, *above,* helps a happy snowman share an important holiday reminder, Christmas is caring.

*Designs: Santa, Barbara Sestok; ornament, Lizzie Kate*

Stitch a fanciful angel ornament with a heartwarming message of holiday love, *above,* on 14-count white Aida cloth.

*Opposite,* even the youngsters enjoy personal holiday decorations. Why not designate a bright-eyed child as an "Elf in Training?"

*Designers: Angel, Robin Kingsley; banner, De Selby*

ELF
in
TRAINING

Capture the wonder of winter with a happy snow couple in holiday attire. Stitch them over one square of 14-count Aida cloth and they're ornament size. Or, stitch over a block of four squares for each chart symbol and they become charming three-dimensional cloth figures to adorn almost any corner.

*Designer: Ursula Michael*

Everybody knows the best Christmas cookies, decked with frosting and sprinkles, come from Mom. Her holiday confections deserve a serving tray that matches the love she bakes into each cookie. For an extra treat, serve a few "cookies," stitched on perforated paper and finished with felt for the tree, too. Then, turn to *page 109* for another cookie-stitching idea.

*Designer: De Selby*

Mom's
Cookie Cafe

*Festive Santa Server*

| Anchor | | DMC |
|---|---|---|
| 002 | • | 000 White |
| 897 | ♥ | 221 Shell pink |
| 403 | ■ | 310 Black |
| 400 | ▲ | 317 Pewter |
| 9046 | ◘ | 321 Christmas red |
| 398 | □ | 415 Pearl gray |
| 358 | ♦ | 433 Chestnut |
| 1022 | ○ | 760 True salmon |
| 1021 | / | 761 Light salmon |
| 271 | I | 819 Pink |
| 881 | – | 945 Ivory |
| 883 | ⊙ | 3064 Cocoa |
| 1024 | ◈ | 3328 Dark salmon |
| 035 | × | 3705 Watermelon |
| 1023 | + | 3712 Medium salmon |
| | ⊕ | 5283 Metallic silver |
| BACKSTITCH | | |
| 403 | / | 310 Black (1X) |
| STRAIGHT STITCH | | |
| 002 | / | 000 White (2X) |
| FRENCH KNOT | | |
| 002 | ○ | 000 White (1X wrapped once) |

***Stitch count:*** *120 high x 100 wide*

***Finished design sizes:***
*14-count fabric – 8¾ x 7⅛ inches*
*16-count fabric – 7½ x 6¼ inches*
*18-count fabric – 6⅔ x 5½ inches*

## Festive Santa Server

### Supplies

*18×20" piece of 14-count white Aida cloth*
*Cotton embroidery floss*
*DMC metallic floss*
*1 additional skein of pearl gray (DMC 415) floss*
*2 additional skeins of white floss*
*½ yard of 45"-wide red rayon velvet fabric*
*⅛ yard of 45"-wide green felted-wool fabric*
*8×10" piece each of fleece and white cotton fabric*
*⅛ yard of white fur with 1¼"-long pile*
*Graph paper*
*Erasable fabric marker*
*Matching sewing thread*
*Tracing paper*
*3×10" piece of cardboard*
*Crafts glue*
*Polyester fiberfill*

*Continued*

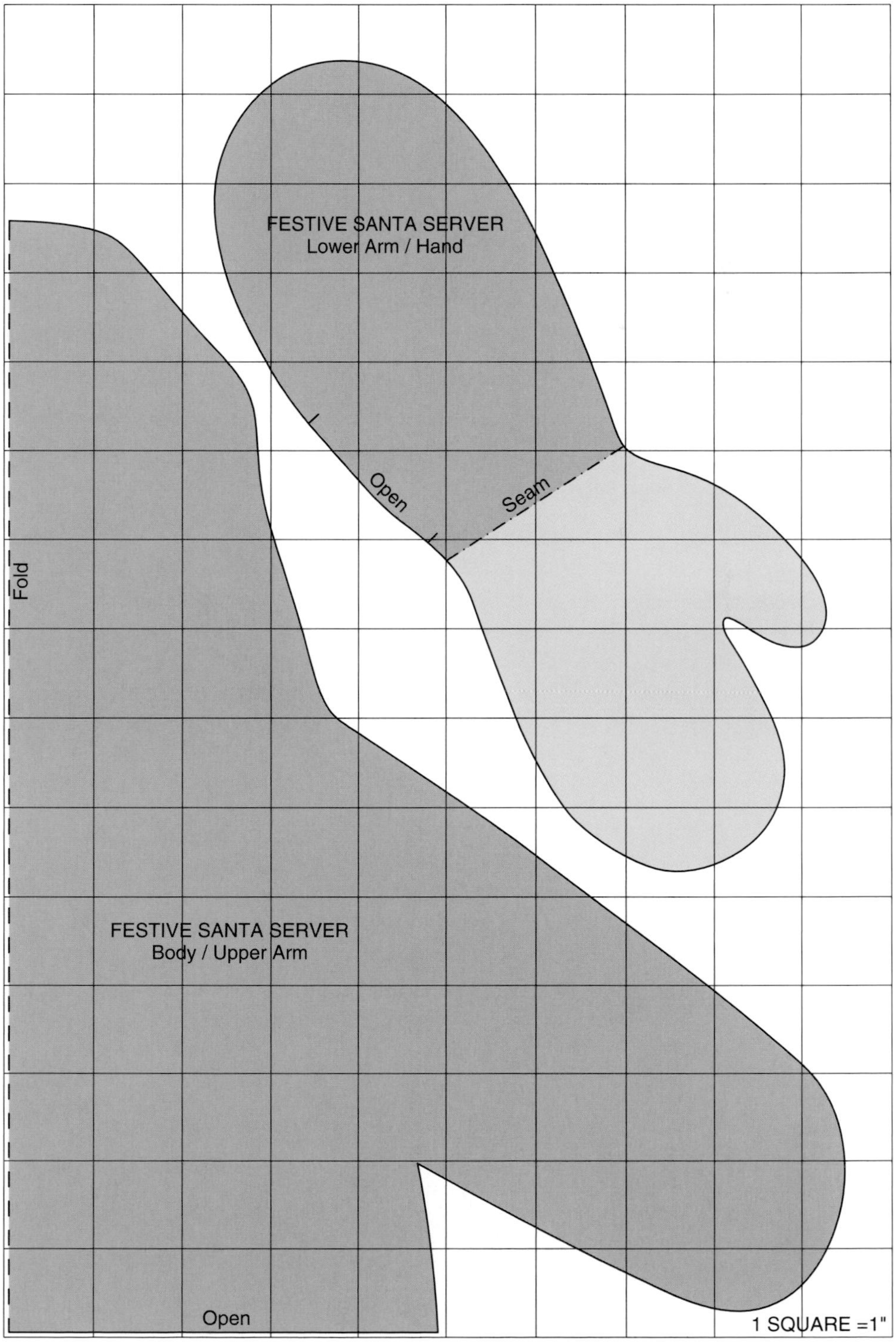

FESTIVE SANTA SERVER
Lower Arm / Hand
Open
Seam
Fold
FESTIVE SANTA SERVER
Body / Upper Arm
Open
1 SQUARE =1"

**Stitches**

Center and stitch the chart on the Aida cloth using three plies of floss unless otherwise specified. Press the stitched piece from the back.

**Assembly**

Centering the design, trim the stitchery to an 8"-wide by 10"-high rectangle. On a flat surface, layer the white fabric and the fleece on the right side of the stitched piece; pin. Working from the wrong side of the stitchery, machine-stitch around the shape ¼" from the edges of the design. Cut a slit through the white fabric *only*. Clip the curves and turn the head right side out through the slit. Press carefully and slip-stitch the opening closed. Set the face aside.

Enlarge the body/upper-arm and the lower-arm/hand patterns on *page 103;* cut out. Fold the velvet in half with right sides together. Use the erasable marker to trace around the outline of the body/upper-arm pattern onto the doubled fabric. Sew along the lines, leaving the bottom edge unstitched. Cut out the shape ½" beyond the stitching. Clip the curves and corners, and turn right side out.

From the velvet fabric, cut out a 4×12" rectangle for the base. Fold the tracing paper in half. Matching the folds, trace around the base pattern, *page 103*. Cut out the paper pattern and unfold. Trace around the shape onto the cardboard; cut out. Center and glue the cardboard oval to the back of the velvet rectangle. Trim the fabric ½" beyond the edge of the board. Fold the raw edges to the back and glue, clipping as needed. Let the glue dry. Stuff the figure firmly with fiberfill. Turn the bottom edge of the figure under ½". Hand-stitch the base to the bottom edge of the figure, adding more fiberfill as needed.

Cut four 6×8" rectangles from the velvet fabric and four 6×7" rectangles from the felted wool. Sew a 6" edge of one red rectangle to the corresponding edge of a green rectangle. Press the seam open. Repeat with the remaining rectangles.

Matching the seams, pin two joined red-green pieces together with right sides facing. Trace the outline of the lower-arm/hand pattern onto the doubled fabric. Sew around the shape on the traced line, leaving an opening for turning. Cut out the shape ½" beyond the outline. Clip the curves and corners, and turn right side out. Stuff the lower-arm/hand firmly and slip-stitch the opening closed. Repeat for the other arm. Set the pieces aside.

From the white fur, cut two 2¾×7" cuffs and one 3×4½" jacket trim piece. (When cutting, use the tip of the scissors to snip through the fabric backing, being careful not to cut the pile on the right side of the fabric.) Position and pin a cuff to each lower arm, centering the fabric over the seam. Turn the edges of the fur under ¼" and slip-stitch in place. Center and pin the jacket trim to the figure with the nap facing down and the bottom edge even with the bottom of the figure. Hand-sew in the same manner as for the cuffs.

With the figure on a table, pin the lower arms to the figure; slip-stitch in place. Position and pin the face on the figure. Hand-sew the face to the figure.

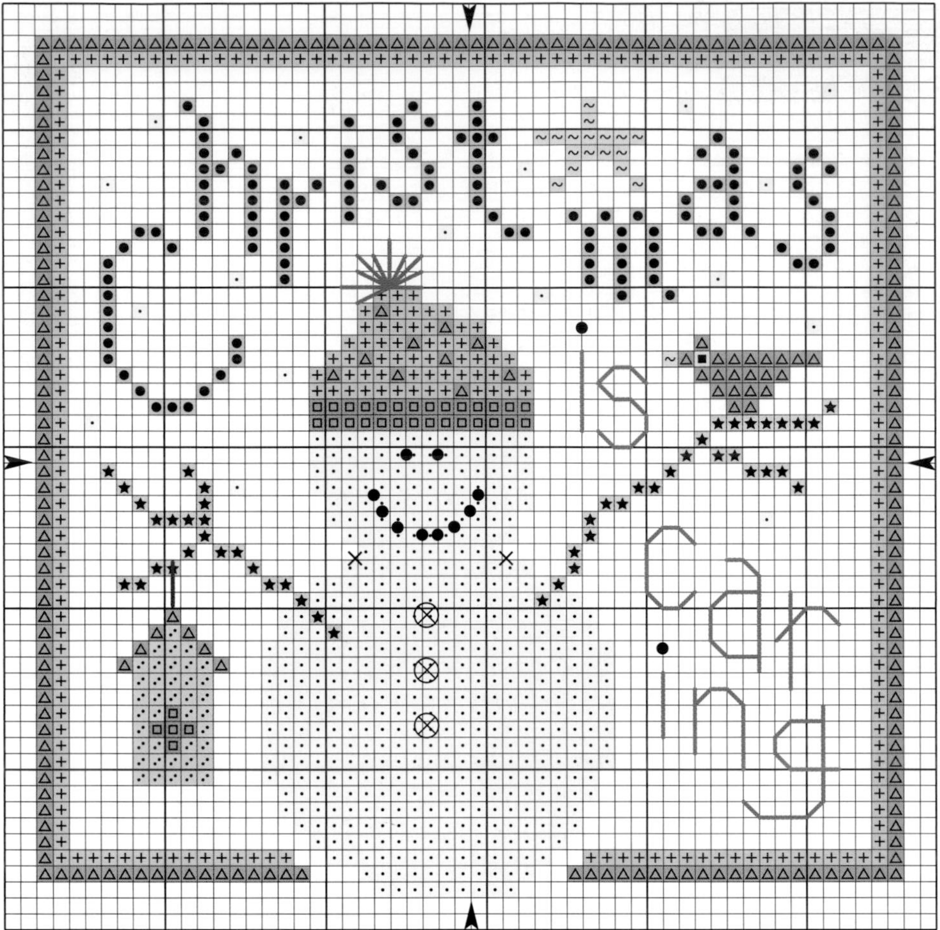

## Christmas Is Caring

**Supplies**

*14" square of 14-count Williamsburg blue Aida cloth*
*Cotton embroidery floss*
*3—⅛"-diameter green buttons*
*4" square of self-stick mounting board with foam*
*18" length of ¼"-wide burgundy flat braid trim*
*6" length of ⅛"-wide burgundy satin ribbon*
*4" square of burgundy felt*
*15" length of ⅞"-wide burgundy ribbon*
*Crafts glue*

**Stitches**

Center and stitch the chart on the Aida cloth using three plies of floss unless otherwise specified.

For the scarf, thread a needle with 12 plies of old gold floss (DMC 727). Insert the needle into the fabric at the X on one side of the snowman's neck. Bring the thread across the back of the fabric and up at the X on the other side of the neck. Tie the floss into a knot at one side of the

## *Christmas Is Caring*

| Anchor | | DMC | |
|---|---|---|---|
| 403 | ■ | 310 | Black |
| 1017 | ⊞ | 316 | Antique mauve |
| 683 | ● | 500 | Blue-green |
| 926 | ⊡ | 712 | Cream |
| 890 | ~ | 729 | Old gold |
| 360 | ★ | 839 | Beige-brown |
| 1035 | ◘ | 930 | Dark antique blue |
| 1033 | ⁖ | 932 | True antique blue |
| 1028 | △ | 3685 | Mauve |

STRAIGHT STITCH (2X)

| | | | |
|---|---|---|---|
| 1035 | / | 930 | Dark antique blue – hanger |
| 1028 | / | 3685 | Mauve – top of cap |

BACKSTITCH (2X)

| | | | |
|---|---|---|---|
| 683 | / | 500 | Blue-green – lettering |

FRENCH KNOT (2X wrapped once)

| | | | |
|---|---|---|---|
| 403 | ● | 310 | Black – eyes and mouth |

SURFACE ATTACHMENTS

| | | | |
|---|---|---|---|
| | ⊗ | | 1/8"- diameter button |
| 890 | × | 727 | Old gold – scarf (12X) |

***Stitch count:*** *54 high x 54 wide*
***Finished design sizes:***
*14-count fabric – 3¾ x 3¾ inches*
*16-count fabric – 3⅓ x 3⅓ inches*
*18-count fabric – 3 x 3 inches*

neck. Trim the floss ends to measure 1". Press the piece from the back.

### Assembly

Peel the protective paper from the mounting board. Center the foam side on the back of the stitchery and press to stick. Trim the excess fabric ½" beyond the edge of the board. Fold the edges of the fabric to the back and glue in place.

Position and glue the braid around the edge of the ornament, overlapping the ends at the top center and trimming the excess. For the hanger, fold the ⅛"-wide ribbon in half to form a loop. Glue the ribbon ends to the top center of the ornament back. Glue the felt to the back.

Tie the ⅞"-wide ribbon in a bow. tack the ribbon to the top center of the ornament. Trim the ribbon ends.

## Snow Couple Figures

*The chart and key are on page 106.*

### Supplies

*For each figure*
*14×16" piece of 14-count Victorian blue Yorkshire Aida cloth*
*Cotton embroidery floss*
*7×10" piece of fusible interfacing*
*⅛ yard of 45"-wide blue-plaid fabric*
*Erasable fabric marking pen*
*½ yard of purchased ⅛"-diameter blue piping*
*Matching sewing thread*
*Plastic pellets*
*Polyester fiberfill*

### Stitches

Center and stitch the chart on the fabric using three plies of floss to work one stitch over a block of four squares for each symbol on the chart. Work the backstitches using one ply. Press the piece from the back.

### Assembly

Fuse the fleece to the wrong side of the stitched piece following manufacturer's instructions. Use the marker to draw a simplified outline just beyond the stitched area. Cut out the shape ½" beyond the outline. Use the stitched piece as a pattern to cut a back from the blue-plaid fabric.

Using the marked line as a guide, sew the piping, raw edges even, around the top and sides of the figure. Sew the front and back together, right sides together, leaving a 3" opening in one side for turning and the bottom edge open. Trim the seams and curves, but *do not* turn.

For the base, fold the tracing paper in half. Matching the fold, trace around the base pattern, *above right,* transferring the dot markings. Cut out the paper pattern and unfold. Trace around the shape onto the blue-plaid fabric, transferring dots; cut out.

Matching side seams to the dots, pin the base to the bottom edge of the figure. Machine-stitch around the oval. Turn the figure right side out through the opening in the side.

Pour plastic pellets into the bottom of the figure to a depth of about 2". Stuff the remainder of the figure with fiberfill. Stitch the opening closed.

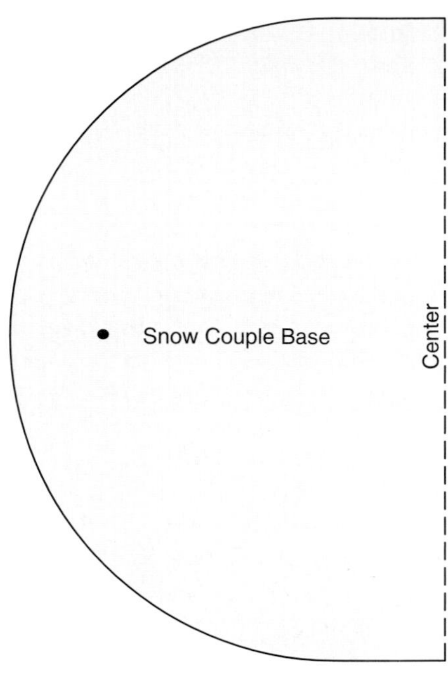


## Snow Couple Ornaments

*The chart and key are on page 106.*

### Supplies

*For each ornament*
*6" square of 14-count Victorian blue Yorkshire Aida cloth*
*Cotton embroidery floss*
*Pinking shears*
*5" square of blue felt*
*Assorted ⅜"- to ½"-diameter buttons*
*14" piece of 18-gauge wire*
*Wire cutters*
*Pencil*
*Awl*

### Stitches

Center and stitch the chart on the fabric using three plies of floss over one square unless otherwise specified. Press the stitched piece from the back.

### Assembly

Centering the design, use pinking shears to trim the stitched Aida cloth to measure 3×4". Use the pinking shears to trim the felt to measure 3⅝×4⅝". Position the stitched Aida atop the felt. Use two plies of black floss (DMC 310) to work running stitches through both layers of fabric three squares from the outer edges of the Aida cloth.

On one side of the ornament, use the awl to pierce a small hole through

*Continued*

the fabric ⅜" from the top and ¾" from the side of the felt. Insert one end of the wire through the back of the ornament to the front. Wrap 2–3" of the wire end around the pencil to form a coil. On the back of the ornament, loosely wrap the wire around the pencil several times. Slip a button onto the wire; then wrap the wire again. Slip a second button onto the wire. Pierce a hole on the other side of the ornament, insert the remaining wire end, and coil as before.

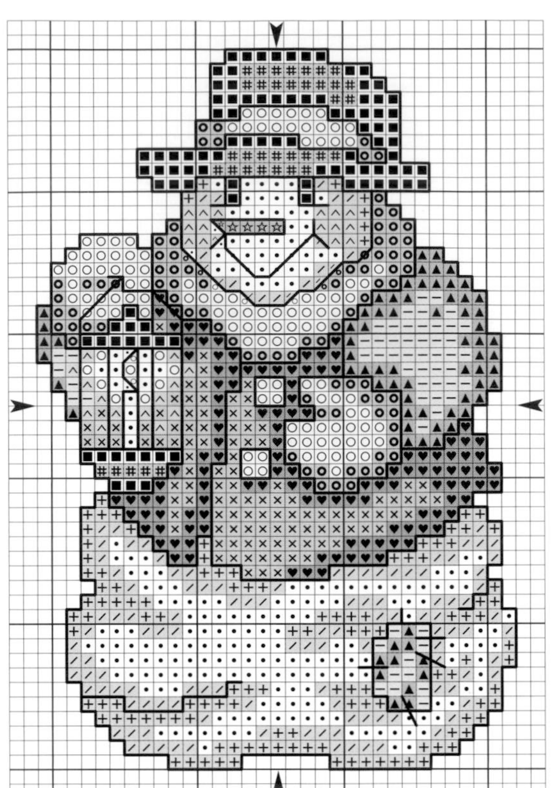

*Snow Couple*

| Anchor | | DMC |
|---|---|---|
| 002 | • | 000 White |
| 403 | ■ | 310 Black |
| 011 | × | 350 Medium coral |
| 401 | # | 413 Pewter |
| 933 | / | 543 Pale beige-brown |
| 332 | ☆ | 608 Orange |
| 295 | ○ | 726 Topaz |
| 1012 | ^ | 754 Peach |
| 307 | ◉ | 783 Christmas gold |
| 131 | ♦ | 798 Dark Delft blue |
| 130 | □ | 809 True Delft blue |
| 013 | ♥ | 817 Deep coral |
| 388 | + | 842 Light beige-brown |
| 246 | ▲ | 986 Dark forest green |
| 243 | – | 988 Light forest green |

BACKSTITCH (1X)

403 / 310 Black – all backstitches

***Snowlady stitch count:*** *49 high x 34 wide*

***Snowlady finished design sizes:***
*14-count fabric – 3½ x 2⅜ inches*
*16-count fabric – 3 x 2⅛ inches*
*18-count fabric – 2¾ x 1⅞ inches*

***Snowlady finished design sizes:***
*7-count fabric – 7 x 4¾ inches*
*8-count fabric – 6⅛ x 4¼ inches*

***Snowman stitch count:*** *50 high x 33 wide*

***Snowman finished design sizes:***
*14-count fabric – 3½ x 2⅓ inches*
*16-count fabric – 3⅛ x 2 inches*
*18-count fabric – 2¾ x 1¾ inches*

***Snowman finished design sizes:***
*7-count fabric – 7⅛ x 4⅝ inches*
*8-count fabric – 6¼ x 4⅛ inches*

# Elf in Training Banner

## Supplies

*16×24" piece of 14-count navy Aida cloth*
*Cotton embroidery floss*
*Erasable fabric marker*
*½ yard of 45"-wide red-print fabric*
*¼ yard of 45"-wide green-print fabric*
*12×14" piece of fleece*
*2 yards of ½"-diameter cording*
*Matching sewing thread*
*7—¼"-diameter gold jingle bells*
*9"-long plastic-wrapped peppermint stick*
*Pleated ribbon*

## Stitches

Center and stitch the chart using three plies of floss unless otherwise specified. Carefully press the stitched piece from the back.

## Assembly

Centering the design, trim the fabric to measure 10×17" high. Use the marker to draw a line across the top of the fabric 2" above the top row of the stitching. Cut away the excess fabric ½" above the line.

To shape the bottom point, fold the fabric in half lengthwise; right sides together. Measure 10½" from the top of the fabric and make a mark on the raw edge of the fabric. At the center fold, measure and

*Continued*

*Elf in Training*

| Anchor | | DMC |
|---|---|---|
| 403 | ■ | 310 Black |
| 9046 | × | 321 True Christmas red |
| 1005 | ♥ | 498 Dark Christmas red |
| 046 | ✱ | 666 Red |
| 923 | ★ | 699 Dark Christmas green |
| 228 | # | 700 Medium Christmas green |
| 227 | ^ | 701 True Christmas green |
| 226 | ○ | 702 Light Christmas green |
| 238 | + | 703 True chartreuse |
| 256 | = | 704 Light chartreuse |
| 301 | ☆ | 744 Medium yellow |
| 300 | / | 745 Light yellow |

BACKSTITCH

403 / 310 Black – all backstitches (1X)

SURFACE ATTACHMENT

○ 6mm jingle bells – cuff points and tip of toe

***Stitch count:*** *100 high x 80 wide*

***Finished design sizes:***
*14-count fabric – 7⅛ x 5¾ inches*
*16-count fabric – 6¼ x 5 inches*
*18-count fabric – 5½ x 4⅜ inches*

ELF
in
TRAINING

mark a point 13¼" from the top. Use a ruler to draw a diagonal line between the marks from the fold to the edge of the fabric. Cut away the excess fabric ½" beyond the diagonal line.

Use the stitched Aida cloth as a pattern to cut a back from the red-print fabric and an interlining piece from the fleece. Also cut six 2×5" hanging tabs from the red-print fabric; round one end of each tab. Set the tabs aside. From the green print fabric, cut enough 1½"-wide strips of the green-print fabric to make 2 yards.

Baste the fleece to the back of the stitched fabric. All measurements include a ¼" seam allowance.

Sew the short ends of the piping strip together to make one long strip. Center the cording lengthwise on the wrong side of the piping strip. Fold the fabric around the cording with the raw edges together. Use a zipper foot to sew through both layers close to the cording.

Baste piping around the sides and rounded end of three of the tab pieces. Sew the tabs together in pairs with right sides together, leaving the top straight edge open. Clip the curves, turn right side out, and press.

Baste piping to the sides and bottom edge of the banner with raw edges even. Position the hanging tabs at the top of the banner with one tab at each end and one tab in the center. Machine-stitch across each tab ¼" from the raw edges.

Sew the front and back together with right sides together, leaving the top straight edge unstitched, and an opening to turn. Trim the seams and clip the corners; turn right side out. Slip-stitch the opening closed; press.

Fold the tabs down to overlap the front of the banner by about 1", and sew a jingle bell on top of each tab through all layers. Sew the remaining jingle bells to the banner at the positions indicated on the chart.

Slip the peppermint stick through the tabs. Thread the ribbon between the peppermint stick and the banner.

## Angel on Heart Ornament

### Supplies

*10" square of 14-count white Aida cloth*
*Cotton embroidery floss*
*DMC metallic embroidery floss*
*Mill Hill petite seed beads*
*Tracing paper*
*Erasable fabric marker*
*10" square of self-stick mounting board with foam*
*16" of 1¼-wide pregathered pink lace*
*⅝ yard of ¼"-diameter white-and-gold cording*
*Crafts glue*

### Stitches

Center and stitch the chart on the Aida cloth using three plies of floss unless otherwise specified. Press the finished stitchery from the back.

### Assembly

Use the erasable marker to draw an outline around the stitched area of the design ¼" beyond the backstitched outline; *do not* cut out. Place the tracing paper over the fabric and trace the drawn outline. Cut out the paper pattern and use it to cut shapes from the mounting board and the felt.

*Angel on Heart Ornament*

| Anchor | | DMC | |
|---|---|---|---|
| 002 | ⊡ | 000 | White |
| 217 | ● | 367 | Medium pistachio |
| 214 | ⊞ | 368 | Light pistachio |
| 1039 | ■ | 518 | Wedgwood blue |
| 303 | ▽ | 742 | Tangerine |
| 301 | ⊓ | 744 | Medium yellow |
| 1012 | ○ | 754 | Peach |
| 1022 | ✱ | 760 | True salmon |
| 1021 | ⊟ | 761 | Light salmon |
| 1024 | ▲ | 3328 | Dark salmon |
| 329 | ⧅ | 3340 | Melon |
| 928 | ⊠ | 3761 | Sky blue |
| 386 | ⊠ | 3823 | Pale yellow |

BACKSTITCH (1X)

| | | | |
|---|---|---|---|
| 217 | / | 367 | Medium pistachio – lettering |
| 360 | / | 898 | Coffee brown – all other stitches |
| 1024 | / | 3328 | Dark salmon – mouth |
| | / | 5282 | Metallic gold – halo |

FRENCH KNOT (1X wrapped twice)

| | | | |
|---|---|---|---|
| 217 | ● | 367 | Medium pistachio – lettering |
| 360 | ● | 898 | Coffee brown – knots on ornaments string |
| 1024 | ● | 3328 | Dark salmon – holly berries |

MILL HILL BEADS

⊙ 40332 Emerald petite glass beads – buttons on dress

***Stitch count:*** *52 high x 59 wide*
***Finished design sizes:***
*14-count fabric – 3¾ x 4¼ inches*
*18-count fabric – 2⅞ x 3¼ inches*

Peel the protective paper from the mounting board. Center the foam side on the back of the stitchery and press to stick. Trim the excess fabric ½" beyond the edge of the board. Fold the edge of the fabric to the back and glue in place.

Cut a 16" length of cord. Position and glue the cord around the edge of the ornament, overlapping the ends at the bottom center and trimming the excess. Glue the lace behind the cord.

For the hanger, fold the remaining cord in half to form a loop. Glue the cord ends to the top center of the ornament back. Glue the felt to the back of the ornament.

## Mom's Cookie Cafe Tray

*The chart and key are on pages 110–111.*

### Supplies

*20×24" piece of 16-count stoney point Aida cloth*
*Cotton embroidery floss*
*17×13" piece of fleece*
*Purchased 17×13" wood tea tray with a 15×11" design area*
*Spray adhesive*
*Crafts glue or tape*

### Stitches

Center and stitch the chart on the Aida cloth. Use three plies of floss to work the stitches unless otherwise specified. Press the stitched piece from the back.

### Assembly

Cut the fleece the same size as the mounting board from the tray. Spray the board lightly with the adhesive and position the fleece on top. Center the wrong side of the stitched piece over the fleece on the board; glue or tape the edges to the back. Assemble the tray following the manufacturer's instructions.

## Mom's Cookie Ornaments

*The chart and key are on pages 110–111.*

### Supplies

*For each ornament*
*4" square of 14-count brown perforated paper*
*Cotton embroidery floss*
*5" square of turquoise felt*
*Crafts glue*
*10" of 1⁄16"-wide white satin ribbon*
*Large-eye needle*

### Stitches

Center and stitch the desired motif from the Mom's Cookie Cafe chart on the perforated paper. Use two plies of floss to work the stitches unless otherwise specified.

### Assembly

Trim the finished stitchery one square beyond the stitched area of the design. Center the stitchery on the felt and glue in place. Trim away the excess felt ⅛" beyond the perforated paper.

For the hanger, use a large needle to thread the ribbon through the felt at the top center of the ornament; knot the ribbon ends.

## Cups for Mom's Cookies

*The chart and key are on pages 110–111.*

### Supplies

*12½×7" piece of 14-count white Aida cloth*
*Cotton embroidery floss*
*Purchased child's Sippie cup*

### Stitches

Center and stitch the desired motifs from the Mom's Cookie Cafe chart on the Aida cloth, leaving eight squares between the motifs. Repeat to achieve a stitched area measuring 7½" wide. Use three plies of floss to work the stitches unless otherwise specified. Press the stitchery from the back.

### Assembly

Trim the finished stitchery ⅝" beyond the stitching on all four sides of the design. Press under ½" on one short edge and both long edges of the stitchery. Insert the design into the cup and snap on the lid.

*Cookies and milk will taste better than ever when the milk is served in cookie-decorated cups.*

Cookie

*Mom's Cookie Cafe*

| Anchor | | DMC | |
|---|---|---|---|
| 002 | · | 000 | White |
| 9046 | ♥ | 321 | Christmas red |
| 358 | ■ | 433 | Dark chestnut |
| 1046 | ✱ | 435 | Light chestnut |
| 362 | I | 437 | Tan |
| 1022 | II | 760 | True salmon |
| 1021 | / | 761 | Light salmon |
| 161 | ◆ | 826 | Bright blue |
| 160 | ⊙ | 827 | Powder blue |
| 186 | ⋈ | 959 | Medium aqua |
| 1020 | ~ | 3713 | Pale salmon |
| 189 | ● | 3812 | Deep aqua |
| 874 | ○ | 3822 | Straw |

BACKSTITCH (1X)

| | | | |
|---|---|---|---|
| 382 | / | 3371 | Black-brown |

***Mom's Cookie Cafe***
***Stitch count:*** *145 high x 195 wide*
***Finished design sizes:***
*14-count fabric – 10⅓ x 14 inches*
*16-count fabric – 9 x 12⅛ inches*
*18-count fabric – 8 x 10⅞ inches*

# *Simply*

# Christmas

*Two keys to creating a memorable Christmas are imagination and a great cross-stitch chart. On the next few pages, you'll find more than a dozen holiday decorations and gifts, all made from one chart and an alphabet.*

W
EL
COM
E
Friends

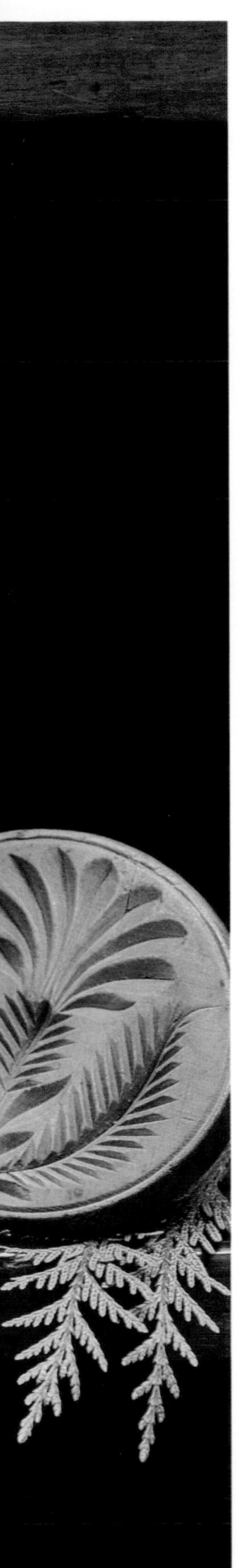

Stitch a gift of words. No matter what the message, when it's charted in this curly alphabet, it will come from the heart. A simple welcome takes the shape of a Christmas tree, *opposite,* and finishes quickly with a premade pillow. A single initial, *above,* becomes the center of attention when stitched with variegated metallic thread and finished as a trinket box. Turn to pages *118, 120, and 125* for more alphabet projects.

*Design: De Selby*

This holiday sampler with its cheery message, *opposite,* is a Christmas treasure trove—a charming addition to your holiday decor plus a springboard for gift and trim ideas. The seven little square motifs in the middle are quick-to-finish ornaments for a tiny tree, *below.* Or, add the garland from the top to a fingertip towel, *right.* Look for more ideas on *pages 118–121.*

*Design: Robin Kingsley*

May this Christmas be bright and merry!
HO
HO
HO

Santa Claus is
Coming to Town

You don't have to read notes to make a musical statement! Use the Welcome Friends alphabet on *page 114* to write the lyrics, punctuate them with motifs from the sampler on *page 117,* and combine them on a colorful wreath, *opposite.*

Look for harmony when adapting motifs from a large piece to smaller projects. The shape of the wreath on the sampler is a happy duet partner for the no-finish jar topper *above.*

## Christmas Sampler

*The chart and key are on pages 122–123.*

**Supplies**

*20×24" piece of 14-count white Aida cloth*
*Cotton embroidery floss*
*One additional skein each of white and dark coffee brown (DMC 898) floss*
*Desired frame*

**Stitches**

Center and stitch the chart using three plies of floss unless otherwise specified. Press from the back.

## Mini Ornaments

*The chart and key are on pages 122–123.*

**Supplies**

*8" square of 14-count white Aida cloth*
*Cotton embroidery floss*
*7/8" squares of thin fleece*
*2" squares of felt in assorted colors*
*White sewing thread*

**Stitches**

Stitch each of the small square motifs from the center of the Christmas Sampler chart on the fabric, separating the shapes by 2". Use three plies of floss unless otherwise specified. Press from the back.

**Assembly**

Cut the motifs apart, leaving as much fabric around each as possible. Center the fleece, then the felt on the wrong side of the stitched piece. Machine-sew the stitched piece and felt together one square beyond the stitched area of the design, sandwiching the fleece between the layers. Trim away the excess Aida cloth and felt three squares beyond the stitched area of the design. Remove the threads from the two outermost rows of Aida cloth on all edges of the stitched piece.

For the hanger, thread the large-eye needle with a 6" six-ply strand of floss that matches the felt. Thread the floss through the corners of the felt on the back of the ornament. Adjust to the desired length and knot each end.

*Combine heart motifs from the Christmas Sampler chart and the Welcome Friends alphabet to make a very special gift. Use the colors from the charts or choose your own.*

## Checkbook Cover

*The charts and keys are on pages 122–124.*

**Supplies**

*Graph paper*
*11×12" piece of 14-count white Aida cloth*
*Graph paper*
*Cotton embroidery floss*
*Purchased checkbook cover kit*
*5¾×6¼" piece of card stock*
*Crafts glue*

**Stitches**

On graph paper outline a horizontal rectangle 83×45 squares. Beginning eight squares from the bottom, center and chart the desired name, separating each letter with one square. Chart the small heart garland from the bottom right corner of the Christmas Sampler two squares above the name, adding motifs, if necessary. Chart the pink and green heart to the left of the garland with the right edge of the backstitch bow touching the garland. Chart the pair of pink hearts to the right of the garland with the left edge one square beyond the garland.

With the 11" edge at the top, fold the fabric in half. Center and stitch the chart on the lower half using three plies of floss unless otherwise specified. Press from the back.

**Assembly**

Remove the mounting paper from the checkbook cover. Position the wrong side of the stitched piece over the paper, centering the design area over the front half of the mounting paper. Trim fabric ½" beyond the mounting paper. Tape or glue the fabric edges to the back. Glue the 5¾×6¼" piece of cardstock to the wrong side of the mounting paper. Insert the design into the checkbook cover.

## Santa Claus Is Coming To Town Wreath

*The charts and keys are on pages 122–124.*

**Supplies**

*Graph paper*
*2—14" lengths of 2"-wide, 16-count red banding with gold trim*
*9×12" piece of 14-count white perforated paper*
*Cotton embroidery floss*
*DMC gold metallic floss (5282)*
*9x12" piece each of white and red stiffened felt*
*Crafts glue*
*Wreath*
*Glue gun and hot-melt adhesive*

**Stitching**

Use the alphabet and graph paper to chart the phrases "Santa Claus is" and "Coming to Town." Center and stitch each phrase on one piece of banding. Use two plies of emerald floss (DMC 910) for the letters and one ply of metallic gold floss for the backstitches.

From the Christmas Sampler chart, stitch one Santa, one tree, one sled, three stockings, and three bells on perforated paper using two plies of floss unless otherwise specified.

**Assembly**

Trim the ends of banding 1½" beyond the stitched area. Turn under ¼" twice; hand-sew in place.

Trim each perforated paper motif one square beyond the stitching. Use the stitched pieces as patterns to cut matching shapes from the white felt. Glue the white felt pieces to the backs of the paper shapes. Glue the shapes onto the red felt, leaving at least ½" between each one. Trim the excess felt ⅛" beyond the perforated paper.

Referring to the photo, *page 118*, as a placement guide, adhere all items to the wreath with hot-melt adhesive.

*Dress a tot in a snowman vest using a portion of the Christmas Sampler chart stitched on large-square fabric.*

## Jar Topper

*The chart and key are on pages 122–123.*

### Supplies

*Purchased green check jar lid cover with 3"-diameter 14-count white Aida cloth insert*
*Cotton embroidery floss*

### Stitches

Center and stitch the wreath chart from the Christmas Sampler on the Aida cloth insert using three plies of floss unless otherwise specified.

## Holly Swag Towel

*The chart and key are on pages 122–123.*

### Supplies

*Purchased 11×18" hunter green velour fingertip towel with a 2½"-wide 14-count Aida cloth insert*
*Cotton embroidery floss*

### Stitches

Center and stitch the holly swag motif from the Christmas Sampler chart on the towel insert using three plies of floss unless otherwise specified.

## Snow People Child's Vest

*The chart and key are on pages 122–123.*

### Supplies

*11" square of 7-count cream Klostern fabric*
*Cotton embroidery floss*
*Child's lined vest pattern with no seams or darts in the front*
*11" square of light blue print fabric*
*¼ yard of bright green print fabric*
*Red print fabric in the amount indicated on the pattern*

### Stitches

Center and stitch the snowman square from the Christmas Sampler chart on the Klostern using six plies for the cross-stitches and two plies for back-stitches, eyelets, and French knots.

### Assembly

Trim the excess Klostern 5 squares beyond the stitching. From the green print, cut 11×4" and 7½×22" rectangles. From the red print, cut 14×20" and 7½×22" rectangles.

Using ½" seam allowances, sew the blue print square to the top edge of the stitched piece. Sew the 11×4" green rectangle to the bottom. Press seams away from the stitched piece. Sew the 4×20" red rectangle to the right of the joined pieces.

Sew the long edges of the 7½×22" red and green rectangles together. Press seam toward the red fabric. Cut in half crosswise. Turn one piece 180°, and sew the two pieces together, forming a checkerboard pattern.

Lay the vest pattern on the fabric block containing the stitched piece and cut it out. Turn the pattern over and place it on the other fabric block; cut out. Cut the vest back and lining from remaining red fabric. If desired, cut the flap from the excess blue fabric. Sew the pieces together, following the pattern instructions.

## Welcome Friends Pillow

*The chart and key are on page 124.*

### Supplies

*8" square of 14-count beige Aida cloth*
*Cotton embroidery floss*
*Mill Hill Crystal Treasures*
*Purchased Tuck A Way pillow with a 6" square opening*

### Stitches

Center and stitch the chart on the Aida cloth using three plies of floss unless otherwise specified.

### Assembly

Centering the design, cut the fabric to measure 7"-square. Carefully tuck the edges of the fabric under the flanges of the pillow.

Using two plies of embroidery floss in a color that harmonizes with the fabric, blanket-stitch the pillow flange to the Aida cloth.

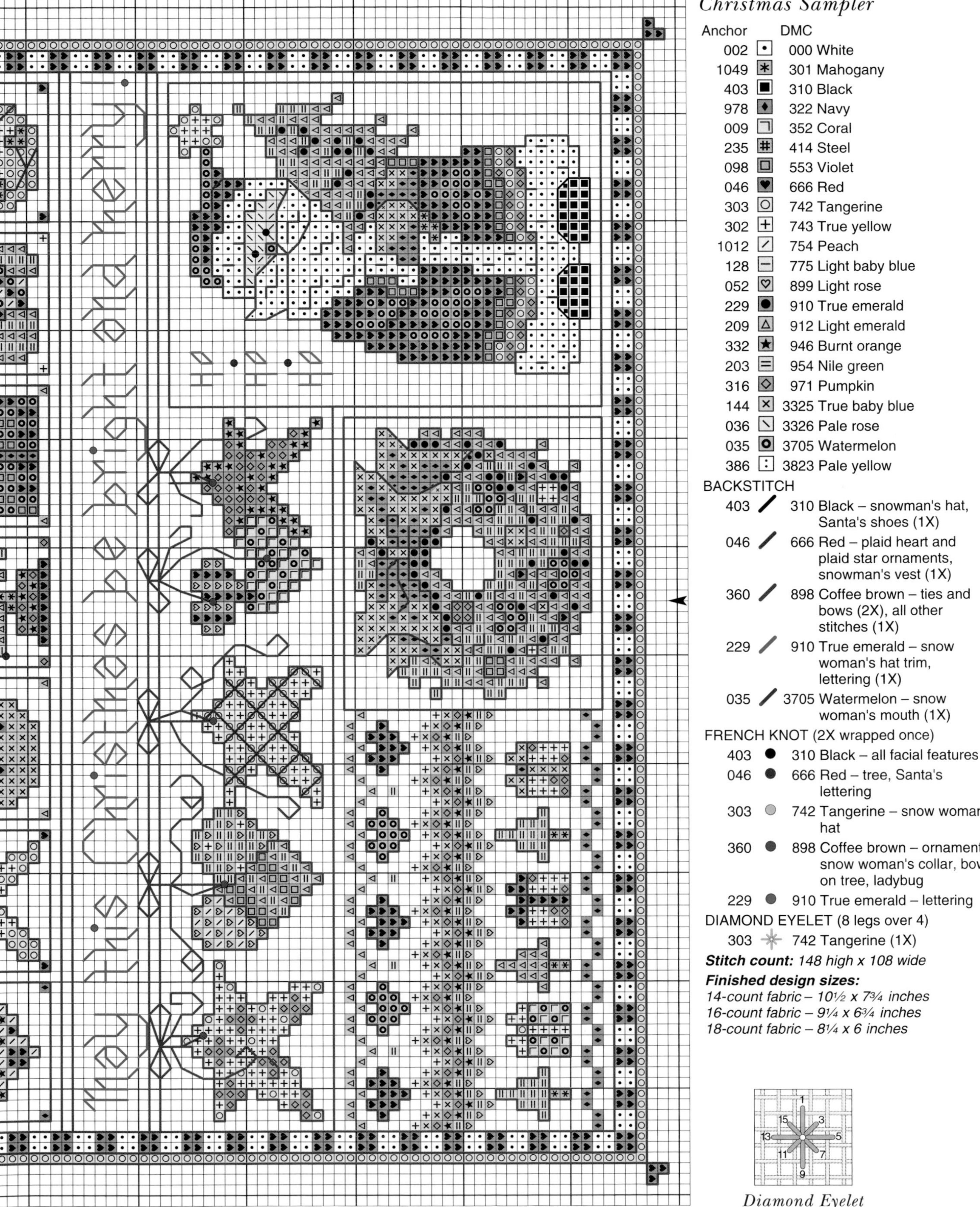

## *Christmas Sampler*

| Anchor | | DMC |
|---|---|---|
| 002 | • | 000 White |
| 1049 | ✱ | 301 Mahogany |
| 403 | ■ | 310 Black |
| 978 | ◆ | 322 Navy |
| 009 | ┐ | 352 Coral |
| 235 | # | 414 Steel |
| 098 | □ | 553 Violet |
| 046 | ♥ | 666 Red |
| 303 | ○ | 742 Tangerine |
| 302 | + | 743 True yellow |
| 1012 | / | 754 Peach |
| 128 | – | 775 Light baby blue |
| 052 | ♡ | 899 Light rose |
| 229 | ● | 910 True emerald |
| 209 | △ | 912 Light emerald |
| 332 | ★ | 946 Burnt orange |
| 203 | = | 954 Nile green |
| 316 | ◇ | 971 Pumpkin |
| 144 | × | 3325 True baby blue |
| 036 | \ | 3326 Pale rose |
| 035 | ◉ | 3705 Watermelon |
| 386 | ⁚ | 3823 Pale yellow |

BACKSTITCH

- 403 / 310 Black – snowman's hat, Santa's shoes (1X)
- 046 / 666 Red – plaid heart and plaid star ornaments, snowman's vest (1X)
- 360 / 898 Coffee brown – ties and bows (2X), all other stitches (1X)
- 229 / 910 True emerald – snow woman's hat trim, lettering (1X)
- 035 / 3705 Watermelon – snow woman's mouth (1X)

FRENCH KNOT (2X wrapped once)

- 403 ● 310 Black – all facial features
- 046 ● 666 Red – tree, Santa's lettering
- 303 ● 742 Tangerine – snow woman's hat
- 360 ● 898 Coffee brown – ornaments, snow woman's collar, bow on tree, ladybug
- 229 ● 910 True emerald – lettering

DIAMOND EYELET (8 legs over 4)

- 303 ✳ 742 Tangerine (1X)

***Stitch count:*** *148 high x 108 wide*

***Finished design sizes:***
*14-count fabric – 10½ x 7¾ inches*
*16-count fabric – 9¼ x 6¾ inches*
*18-count fabric – 8¼ x 6 inches*

*Diamond Eyelet*

*Welcome Friends*

| Anchor | | DMC | |
|---|---|---|---|
| 1005 | ■ | 816 | Garnet (2X) |
| 1044 | ■ | 895 | Hunter green (2X) |

SATIN STITCH (3X)

1206 / 115 Garnet variegated floss

SURFACE ATTACHMENTS

X 12175 Mill Hill Red bright large flat star

***Stitch count:*** *75 high x 75 wide*
***Finished design sizes:***
*14-count fabric – 5⅓ x 5⅓ inches*
*16-count fabric – 4⅝ x 4⅝ inches*
*18-count fabric – 4⅛ x 4⅛ inches*

## Initial Box

### Supplies

*8" square of 10-count chili pepper Heatherfield fabric*
*Kreinik misty scarlet (1400) Ombre thread*
*Kreinik silver (001) #8 fine braid*
*4½"-diameter round papier mâché box with picture frame insert*
*¼ yard of burgundy print fabric*
*⅛ yard of burgundy felt*
*2¾" circle of thick batting*
*Erasable fabric marking pen*
*½ yard of ½"-wide silver braid*
*10" of 3⁄16"-diameter silver sew-in cording*
*Crafts glue*

### Stitches

Center and stitch one initial from the Welcome Friends chart on the fabric. Use one strand of thread for all cross-stitches and backstitches.

### Assembly

From burgundy print, cut a 3×14¼" rectangle for box sides, a 1⅛×14¼" rectangle for lid sides, and an 8"-diameter circle for box top. From the burgundy felt, cut a 1¾×12½" rectangle for lining sides and three 4¼"-diameter circles for the lid lining, the lining bottom, and the box bottom.

Trace the opening in the box lid on the inner cardboard circle. Remove the inner cardboard circle from the lid. Center the batting on the drawn circle and glue. Center the lid over the stitched initial. Use the erasable marker to trace around the lid on the fabric. Cut out just inside the drawn line. Center the stitched piece over the batting. Lift the edges of the stitched piece, spread glue on the portion of the cardboard not covered by batting, and press the fabric into the glue, pulling fabric as tightly over fleece as possible. Glue one burgundy felt circle to the other side of the cardboard circle. Set aside.

Fold one short edge of the 3×14¼" burgundy print rectangle under ¼". Spread glue on the outer sides of the box. Starting with the unfolded short edge of the rectangle, wrap it around the box, centering it on the sides of the box with the excess fabric extending above the rim and below the bottom by about ½". Overlap the folded edge to cover the raw edge. Press the fabric to stick and smooth it. Apply glue to the wrong side of the fabric at the top rim of the box, fold it to the inside, and press to stick. Apply glue to the fabric at the bottom and press it to the bottom of the box, folding small, evenly spaced tucks into the fabric as you work.

Apply glue to the back of the 1¾×12½" felt rectangle and press it to the inside walls of the box with one long edge aligned with the top edge of the box. Trim ⅛" from the edges of the remaining two felt circles. Apply glue to one of the circles and press it to the inside bottom of the box. Apply glue to the the other circle, and press it to the bottom of the box.

Center the box lid, rim up, on the wrong side of the burgundy print circle. Use the erasable marker to trace around the inner opening. Cut out ½" inside the drawn line. Clip at ¼" intervals from the cut edge to the drawn line. Apply glue to the wrong side of the fabric and press it to the lid, folding the clipped edge to the inside. Smooth the fabric at the outer edge to the sides of the lid's rim, folding small, evenly spaced tucks into the fabric as you work. Then fold the remaining fabric to the inner sides of the rim.

Fold both the long edges and one short edge of the burgundy print 1⅛×14¼" rectangle under ¼". Apply glue to the back of the fabric. Starting with the raw edge, press the fabric to the lid's rim, overlapping the folded short edge to cover the raw edge. Center the braid on the rim and glue. Clip the sew-in tape of the silver cording at ¼" intervals, creating tabs. Position the cording around the inner opening of box lid, overlapping the ends. Glue the tabs to the inside of the box lid.

Trim any felt that extends beyond the edge of the cardboard circle. Insert the circle into the box lid so the stitched piece shows through the circular opening.

## Flannel Stockings

### Supplies

*Graph paper*
*¼ yard of 2¾"-wide 30-count medium blue/dark blue Kristen or 3⅛"-wide 27-count natural Celeste linen banding*
*Cotton embroidery floss*
*¼ yard of cotton flannel*
*Fusible fleece*
*Matching thread*
*1¼ yards of ⅛"-wide satin ribbon (optional)*

### Stitches

Chart the desired name using the Welcome Friends alphabet and separating letters with one square. Fold the banding in half crosswise. On one half, center and stitch the name using three plies of a floss color that coordinates with the cotton flannel.

### Assembly

Enlarge the stocking pattern on *page 66*. Add a 2¼" facing to the top of the pattern. Cut two stocking pieces from flannel. Cut one from fleece, omitting the 2¼" facing.

Fuse the fleece to the back of the stocking front. With right sides together, sew the stocking front and back together using ½" seam allowance. Trim and clip seam allowance and turn right side out.

Fold under ¼" along the top edge of the stocking and topstitch through both layers. Fold the top of the stocking to the inside another 2" and tack in place.

Measure the width of the stocking at the top and add 1". Cut the banding to this length. Overcast the cut edges of the banding to prevent fraying and sew the short ends together using a ½" seam. Slip the banding over the stocking top and topstitch in place. If desired, cut the ribbon in half and thread each piece through the eyelets in the banding. Tie the ends in a bow.

*Need a last-minute gift? Use the swirly alphabet,* opposite, *to stitch a name on prefinished banding and sew up an easy flannel stocking.*

# Cross-Stitch Basics

### Getting started

For most projects in this book, the starting point is at the center. Every chart has arrows that indicate the horizontal and vertical centers. With your finger, trace along the grid to the point where the two centers meet. Compare a symbol at the center of the chart to the key and choose which floss color to stitch first. To find the center of the fabric, fold it into quarters and finger-crease or baste along the folds with a single ply of contrasting floss.

Cut the floss into 15" to 18" lengths, and separate all six plies. Recombine the plies as indicated in the project instructions, and thread them into a blunt-tip needle.

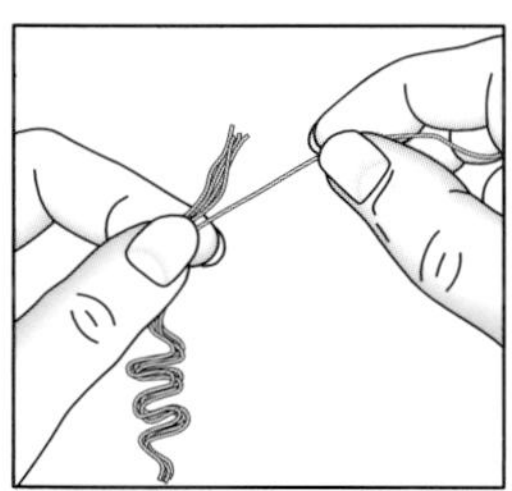

*Separating Floss*

### Basic cross-stitch

Make one cross-stitch for each symbol on the chart. For horizontal rows, stitch the first diagonal of each stitch in the row. Then work back across the row, completing each stitch. On most linen and even-weave fabrics, work your stitches over two threads as shown in the diagram below. For Aida cloth, each stitch fills one square.

You also can work cross-stitches in the reverse direction. Just remember to embroider the stitches uniformly—that is, always work the top half of each stitch in the same direction.

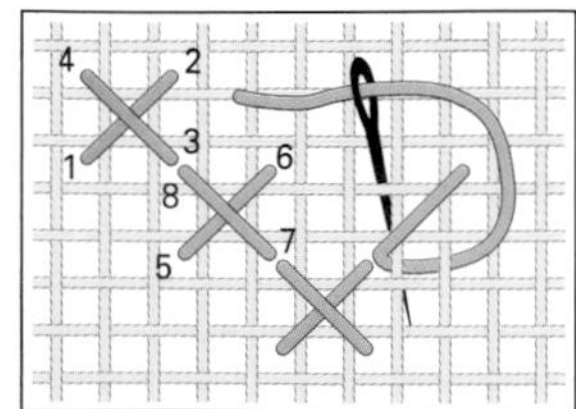


*Cross-Stitch Worked Singly*

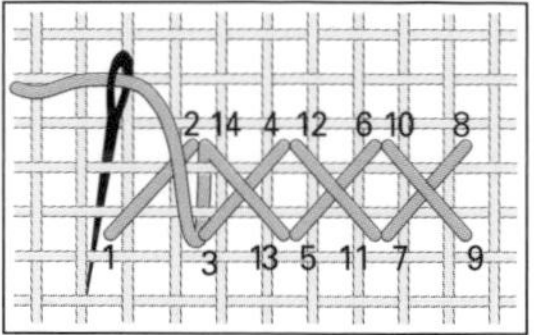


*Cross-Stitch Worked in Rows*

### To secure thread at the beginning

The most common way to secure the beginning tail of the thread is to hold it in place on the back side while working the first four or five stitches over it.

To secure the thread with a waste knot, thread the needle and knot the end of the thread. Insert the needle from the right side of fabric, about 4 inches away from the first stitch. Bring the needle up through the fabric, and work the first series of stitches. When finished, clip the knot on the right side. Rethread the needle with excess floss and push the needle through to the stitches on the wrong side of the fabric.

When you work with two, four, or six plies of floss, use a loop knot. Cut half as many plies of thread, but make each one twice as long. Recombine the plies, fold the strand in half, and thread all of the ends into the needle. Work the first diagonal of the first stitch, then slip the needle through the loop formed by folding the thread.

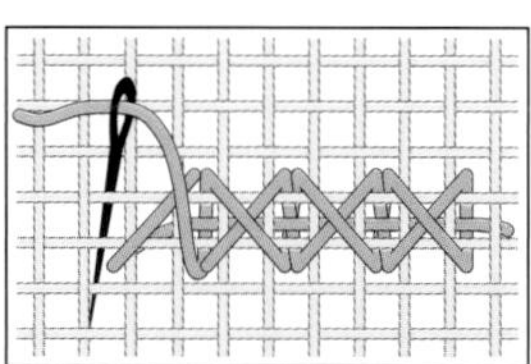

*To Secure Thread at the Beginning*

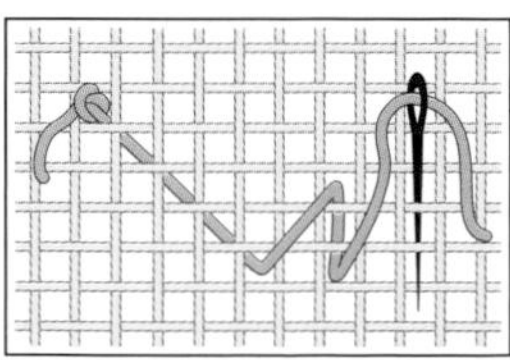

*To Secure Thread with a Waste Knot*

### To secure thread at the end

To finish, slip the threaded needle under previously stitched threads on the wrong side of the fabric for four or five stitches, weaving the thread back and forth a few times. Clip the thread.

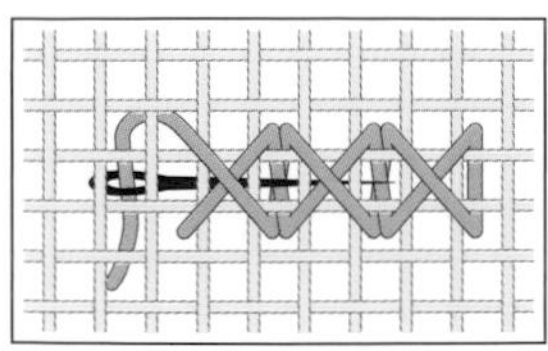

*To Secure Thread at the End*

### Quarter and three-quarter cross-stitches

To obtain rounded shapes in a design, use quarter and three-quarter cross-stitches. On linen and evenweave fabrics, a quarter cross-stitch will extend from the corner to the center intersection of the threads. To make quarter cross-stitches on Aida cloth, estimate the center of the square. Three-quarter cross-stitches combine a quarter cross-stitch with a half cross-stitch. Both stitches may slant in any direction.

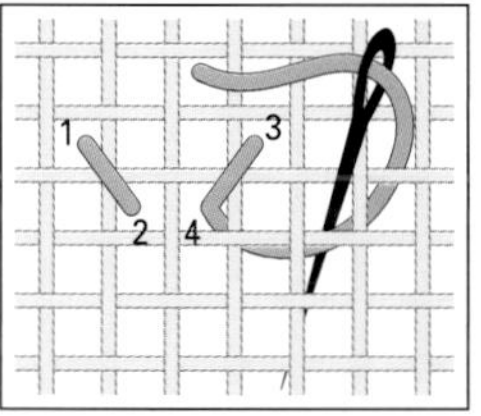


*Quarter Cross-Stitch*

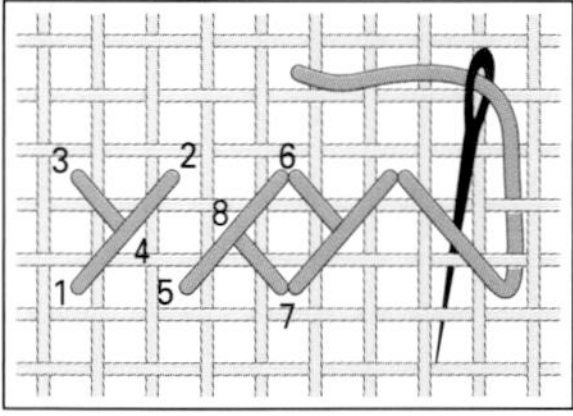


*Three-Quarter Cross-Stitch*

### Backstitches

Backstitches define and outline the shapes in a design. For most projects, backstitches require only one ply of floss. On the color key, (2X) indicates two plies of floss, (3X) indicates three plies, etc.

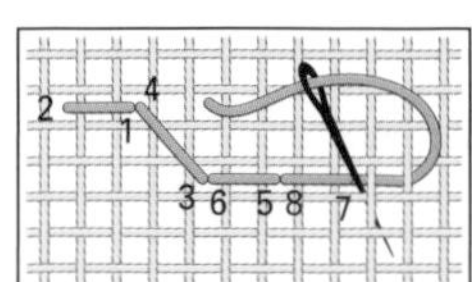


*Backstitch*

# Index

# Sources

*Many of the materials and items used in this book are available at crafts and needlework stores. For more information, write or call the manufacturers listed below.*

**SPIRIT OF THE SEASON**

**Roses Box and Pin,** *pages 8–9:* Lugana fabric and Damask Aida cloth—Wichelt Imports, Inc., Rte. 1, Stoddard, WI 54658, www.wichelt.com; Zweigart, 2 Riverview Dr., Somerset, NJ 08873-1139, www.zweigart.com, 732/271-1949. Oak box—Sudberry House, Box 895, Old Lyme, CT 06371.

**Angel with Mandolin,** *page 10:* Cashel linen—Zweigart.

**Striped Ornament Jar,** *page 11:* Aida cloth—Wichelt Imports, Inc.; Zweigart. Brass trinket jar—Mill Hill, 800/447-1332.

**Partridge Wreath,** *page 12:* Jubilee fabric—Zweigart. Jo Sonya Artist's Colors—Chroma, Inc., 205 Bucky Dr., Lititz, PA 17543, www.chroma-inc.com, 800/257-8278. Crown plate frame—Sudberry House.

**Merry Christmas,** *page 13:* Aida cloth—Wichelt Imports, Inc.; Zweigart.

**Fruit, Holly, and Mistletoe Arch,** *page 14:* Janina fabric—Zweigart.

**Apple Wreath Ornament.** *page 15:* Linen—Zweigart.

**Poinsettia Wreath,** *page 16:* Quaker cloth—Zweigart.

**HOMESPUN HOLIDAYS**

**Feather Tree Ornament,** *page 30:* Linaida fabric—Charles Craft, P.O. Box 1049, Laurinburg, NC 28253, www.charlescraft.com.

**Folk-Art Kitchen Accessories,** *page 31:* Linen banding and Checker ribbon—Mill Hill.

**Holiday House Ornament,** *page 32:* Linen—Wichelt Imports, Inc.

**Christmas Star Ornament,** *page 33:* Linen—Wichelt Imports, Inc.

**Holly Vest,** *page 34:* Tula fabric—Zweigart.

**Holiday Heart Mittens,** *page 35:* Mittens—Aris Isotoner, 417 5th Ave., New York, NY, 10016. RibbonFloss—Rhode Island Textile Company, P.O. Box 999, Pawtucket, RI 02862-0999.

**Christmas Sheep Needle Roll and Ornament,** *page 35:* Linen—Zweigart. Aida cloth—Wichelt Imports, Inc.; Zweigart. Overdyed floss—The Gentle Art, 4081 Bremo Recess, New Albany, OH 43054, e-mail: gentleart@aol.com, 614/855-8346. Sheep button—Shepherd's Bush, 220 24th Street, Ogden, UT 84401, 801/399-4546. Ribbon—C.M. Offray & Sons, Inc., Route 24, Box 601, Chester, NJ 07930, 908/879-4700.

**Hearts Come Home Album,** *page 36:* Linen—Wichelt Imports, Inc.

**STOCKINGS AND STUFFERS**

**Holiday Borders Stocking,** *page 48:* Annabelle and Jubilee fabric—Zweigart.

**Bell Shelf Trim,** *page 49:* Aida banding with crocheted edging—Zweigart.

**Snowman and Gingerbread Pin Cushions,** *page 49:* Tiny Tuck pillows—Olde Colonial Designs, P.O. Box 704 Marshfield, MA 02050, 781/826-3447.

**Highland Santa Pillow,** *page 50:* Cornerblock fabric—Charles Craft. Pillow form—Fairfield Processing Corp., P.O. Box 1157, Danbury, CT 06813, www.poly-fil.com.

**Tartan Border Breadcover,** *page 50:* Breadcloth—Charles Craft.

**Highland Santa Stocking,** *page 51:* Linaida cloth—Charles Craft. Jingle bells—Darice Inc., 21160 Drake Rd., Strongsville, OH 44136-6699.

**Let It Snow Stockings,** *pages 52–53:* Jobelan fabric—Wichelt Imports, Inc.

**Pocket Pals Dolls,** *page 54:* Polyester fiberfill and plastic pellets—Fairfield Processing Corp.

**Quilt Block Chatelaine,** *page 58:* Aida banding—Zweigart.

**Tree and Snowflake Paperweight,** *page 59:* Linen—Wichelt Imports, Inc.; Zweigart. Paperweight—Yarn Tree Designs, 117 Alexander St., P.O. Box 724, Ames, IA 50010, 800/247-3952.

**Thistle Earrings,** *page 63:* Button forms—Prym-Dritz Corp., P.O. Box 5028, Spartanburg, SC 29304, www.dritz.com.

**Little Lamb Sleeper and Booties,** *page 63:* Waste canvas—Zweigart. Booties—Charles Craft.

**ALL THAT GLITTERS**

**Old World Santa and Pillow,** *pages 72–73:* Natural and Betsy Ross linen—Wichelt Imports, Inc.

**Holly and Hardanger Star Ornament,** *page 74:* Belfast linen—Zweigart.

**Jingle Bell Ornament,** *page 74:* Monaco fabric—Charles Craft.

**Madonna and Child Ornament,** *page 75:* Aida cloth—Wichelt Imports, Inc.; Zweigart.

**Father Christmas Tree Skirt and Package Ties,** *page 76–77:* Tilla tree skirt—Zweigart. Perforated paper—Yarn Tree Designs.

**Winter Holiday Wreath,** *page 78:* Linen—Wichelt, Inc. Tray—Sudberry House.

**Candle and Holly Ornament,** *page 79:* Aida cloth—Wichelt Imports, Inc.

**French Horn Ornament,** *page 80:* Edinburgh linen—Zweigart.

**WINTER WHIMSY**

**Festive Santa Server,** *page 94:* White fur fabric—Monterey Inc., 1725 Delavan Dr., Janesville, WI 53546, www.monterey outlet.com, 800/432-9959. Polyester fiberfill and plastic pellets—Fairfield Processing Inc.

**Christmas Is Caring Ornament,** *page 95:* Aida cloth—Wichelt Imports, Inc. Ribbon—Midori, 1432 Elliot Ave. W, Seattle, WA 98119.

**Elf in Training Banner,** *page 97:* Aida cloth—Wichelt Imports, Inc.; Zweigart. Jingle bells—Darice Inc. Ribbon—MKB/Mokuba, www.festivegiftwrap.com, 212/302-5010.

**Snow Couple Ornaments and Figures,** *page 98–99:* Yorkshire Aida cloth—Wichelt Imports, Inc.; Zweigart. Polyester fiberfill and plastic pellets—Fairfield Processing Inc.

**Mom's Cookie Ornaments,** *page 100:* Perforated paper—Yarn Tree Designs.

**Mom's Cookie Cafe Tray,** *page 101:* Aida cloth—Wichelt Imports, Inc. Tray—Sudberry House.

**Cups for Mom's Cookies,** *page 109:* Sippie-cups—Charles Craft.

**SIMPLY CHRISTMAS**

**Welcome Friends Pillow,** *page 114:* Aida cloth—Wichelt Imports, Inc.; Zweigart. Tuck A Way pillow—Olde Colonial Designs

**Initial Box,** *page 115:* Heatherfield fabric—Wichelt Imports, Inc. Papier mâché box—Decorator & Craft Corp., 428 S. Zelta, Wichita, KS 67207, 316/685-6265.

**Mini Ornaments,** *page 116:* Perforated paper—Yarn Tree Designs.

**Holly Swag Towel,** *page 116:* Fingertip towel—Charles Craft.

**Santa Claus is Coming to Town Wreath,** *page 118:* Stiffened Easy Felt—Consumer Products Enterprises, Inc., 541 Buffalo/West Springs Highway, Union, SC 29379; www.cpe-felt.com, 800/427-7900.

**Jar Topper,** *page 119:* Charles Craft.

**Checkbook Cover,** *page 120:* Checkbook cover—Yarn Tree Designs.

**Snow People Child's Vest,** *page 121:* Klostern fabric—Zweigart.

**Flannel Stockings,** *page 125:* Linen banding—Mill Hill.

**Threads:** Anchor, Consumer Service Dept., P.O. Box 12229, Greenville, SC 29612, www.coatsandclark.com; DMC, Port Kearney Bldg. 10, South Kearney, NJ 07032-0650, www.dmc-usa.com; Kreinik Manufacturing Co., Inc., www.kreinik.com, 800/537-2166.